NOT YOUR AVERAGE

by Joseph E. Prince

Edited by
Colette and Jerry Price
and Trinan Verwys

NOT YOUR AVERAGE

by Joseph E. Prince

Edited by
Colette and Jerry Price
and Trinan Verwys

Not Your Average Joe

ISBN: 979-8-9886465-5-6   Softbound

ISBN: 979-8-9886465-6-3   EBook

ISBN: 979-8-9886465-7-0   Hardbound

Request for information should be addressed to: Curry Brothers Marketing and Publishing Group

P.O. Box 247 Haymarket, VA 20168

Cover Design: Alya Hurych

Executive Editing: Tiffany Tillman

CURRY BROS.
MARKETING + PUBLISHING GROUP

TABLE OF CONTENTS

A front row seat
to the history of a young man
and his journey with autism.

THE STING

———————◆———————

Chapter 1

Busted!

BERLIN, 1936: The immortal Jesse Owens is crouched at the starting line. He's about to make one of the most famous runs in the history of track and field. But in this race, Owens' greatest competition is not the Nazi faithful in attendance. It is not German ruler, Adolf Hitler.

His greatest competition is Joe Prince. I am ready to beat Jesse Owens. There I am, in the midst of that black and white backdrop, in the starting block right next to Owens. I almost touch him. Owens is crouched at the starting line. He takes a deep breath and swallows hard, then his head relaxes for the "Set" command from the official starter. I have seen this routine thousands of times, and I follow suit. I also settled, take a deep breath, gulp, and then relax.

"SET!"

We hear the command and act accordingly. We come to our set positions, the world and Olympic records on the line. The starting gun explodes, and almost instantly so do we, blasting from the starting line nearly at the same time.

Suddenly, the glare of a dozen headlights surrounds me. BUSTED! And just as suddenly, my Olympic vision fades.

FRESNO, CALIF., 1974: Nobody says anything to me as I walk back to the starting line to pick up my blocks and return to my dorm room. I already know that I'm going to be in big trouble when Coach Cockerham sees me tomorrow. The headlights disappear, and I sort of wish I could disappear for a couple of days, too. Coach wasn't there in person, but I am certain that within a very short time the full report will be in his hands.

Eleven-thirty at night is not going to sound like a good time to be training, especially since I have been nursing a torn Achilles' tendon along with some significant discomfort in the lower part of my stomach. I am usually able to ignore the pain, since I've had problems off and on with flu-like symptoms in my stomach and intestines for some time going back as far as my high school days. Even though this time it seems to be much worse, I have decided that it's no big deal, just pain left from that kick in the groin I got a couple of months ago in a pick-up basketball game. But add the Achilles' problem, and my training had gotten close to zero.

There I was, Joe Prince, ready to become the next world record holder in the 100 meters (in MY mind at least), and something like a torn Achilles' or other pain should not be holding me up. Come on, an athlete has to just live with a little pain, right? Coaches had detected that I was injured and had ordered me to do nothing, but that was like taking water from a thirsty man. Don't try to stop me!

In a way, it seemed I was always chasing record in the 100, whether it was Jesse Owens in my late-night dreams, or Jim Farmer at Fresno Pacific. But more on that later. First a little background on my track career.

At 20 years old, I just come off a super year running at Cal Poly SLO (San Luis Obispo), where I made the 1974 NCAA All-American team as a sprinter in my first year of university competition. I had also been the CCAA (California Collegiate Athletic Association) champion in the 220.

However, after transferring to Fresno Pacific, things were not going as I had planned. Reality hit me full force some six months before when I got my grades from the spring quarter at Cal Poly. I was just not cut out to be a great student.

After looking into attending a couple of other well-known track schools, I transferred to Fresno Pacific, because I felt my chances academically would be much better there. My academic struggles were well documented, and I knew after my first full year of college that I needed more help than I could get at Cal poly. I wanted so much to graduate, so I could be the first Prince with a college degree. Fresno Pacific was the one place I felt confident that I would get all the individual help I might want. It was a much smaller school an NAIA college of less than 400 students. As an added bonus, it was a Christian college, which I knew would please my folks as well.

When I talked with Coach Bill Cockerman, he impressed me as a really likable man, the type you instantly felt you could trust. He could make you believe you were the most important person in the world, expressing a personal care and concern for each one of his athletes. He made me feel so confident and secure, that I took an immediate liking to him, and was excited about the prospect of being on his team. I was the first full scholarship track athlete in Fresno Pacific history, and I was convinced that soon I would be breaking school records in more than one event.

I would start by chasing Farmer's 100-yard record of 9.4 set five years earlier. I figured the 220 record would come in its own due time, since I had already run faster than their current best. The 100 would be my ultimate prize, the icing on the cake, so to speak. However, my starts were really slow, so I would need plenty of work on them. I was more than happy to work as many hours as necessary to make them better. But how could I improve if I couldn't practice? That's why I decided to take matters into my own hands. And why late-night runs seem like a good idea at the time.

So here I was, reduced to sneaking around at night in order to work on starts in a covert effort to practice as much as I could. How could I break those records if I didn't train? Coach probably was suspicious of me, since I'd been hobbling around for over two weeks, and then the Achilles' injury should have shown at least a LITTLE improvement. Instead, I was worse than before, and it really didn't take a genius to figure out what I was doing something wrong.

So he had set me up! Naturally, I was upset with him doing it, but I wasn't going to get my say when he showed up. He'd be doing all the talking the next day. Even after I went to bed, I didn't sleep well the rest of the night, dreading the moment I'd have to face him.

It wasn't because he was the scolding sort. That wasn't Coach Cockerham's style. Instead, it was a feeling of shame. He was so trusting and honest that no one ever wanted to go against him. I felt really guilty because I thought I had let him down.

When we finally met, I gave him a long puppy-dog face, but it had no effect. I thought it might make him feel sorry for me, at least just a little, but he didn't buy into it.

"Princer, when you finish breakfast, we're going to see Dr. Stone."

So my long face hadn't helped a bit. And I knew what "Dr. Stone" meant. I was going to get a cast on my foot. Sure enough, within a couple of hours I sat glumly and watched as the cast was molded around my foot.

At the time, I had no idea that would be the least of my worries. It was too bad they couldn't fix my stomach pain just as easily.

I hated every minute of imprisonment in that cast, and was so happy when it finally came off. It had been on for about six weeks, which was at least five weeks too long for me. Now I had only about two weeks to get ready and run an indoor meet or two, but at least I could get back to the training again. Seemed easy enough at the time. But those annoying cramps in my lower abdomen just wouldn't go away.

When the cast went on, I had lots of time to think, and more and more I was aware that something wasn't right, because there were times I just doubled up with pain. It really bothered me. I was actually willing to go to the doctor without arguing back. We had been to two doctors already, and it was getting to be time to see specialist. Because I was back running in the indoor track season, I figured I could put it off just a little longer.

Even though I only had one indoor, I did well, placing second in the 60-yard dash in a time of 6.3. We felt that it was respectable considering how little training I had done.

But just a few days before the outdoor season was ready to begin, I found myself in yet another doctor's office, to get another diagnosis. I didn't like what he had to say.

"Joey, you're not going to want to hear this, but I need to get you in the hospital for some tests this Thursday," said Dr. Kamman. "I don't like what I see and the lumps that I'm finding, so perhaps we need to go a step further to see what is going on."

I felt sure that he knew what was going on, and that surgery was going to be a part of it. In my mind, that meant he would be cutting me up and poking around. Actually, his original intention had been only to take some tissue for a biopsy, but I didn't know that at the time.

In a fog, I drove back to school. I had no conscious memory of the six-mile drive back to campus. That is, until the honking horns made me aware of the descending arms of the barriers of the railroad crossing.

I was so scared by what the doctor had told me, that I went directly to coach Cockerman's house. He was not there, but his wife Judy let me in to wait for him. He finally arrived.

"Coach, Dr. Kamman just told me that I may need some kind of tests or surgery on Thursday and we have a meet on Saturday. What are we going to do?" Of course "we" actually meant what was he going to do.

I was so unnerved that I was shaking inwardly, but trying hard not to let it show on the surface.

"You've got to call this man and tell him that I have to run. At least convince him that I need to run the first meet!"

I was trying to be as dramatic as I could to get coach on my side. I was almost demanding that he makes something happen. Calls were made, and after negotiations proceeded back and forth for a while, it was agreed that I could run in the meet on Saturday if I would PROMISE to submit myself to Sierra Hospital no later than 3:00 pm the following day. I don't think that either Coach or Dr. Kamman thought it was best for me, but they knew that I could be a stubborn as anyone in the world when I set my mind on something. Allowing me to run one meet was their small concession to a mule-head!

The day of the race arrives. I am busy along with the other runners, setting our blocks and taking practice starts. In the bleachers I can see Coach Cockerman, but he has a frown on his face. I can just imagine how he might be thinking about whether it was right to let me run. He is shaking his head, probably thinking what a problem I am to him. I'm determined not to let him down, so I return my concentration to the race.

I was trying as much as possible to take my mind off the pain and cramps. I couldn't, no wouldn't, let it interfere. Not today. But as I walked to the starting blocks, I felt a stabbing pain that was so sharp it took my breath away. I bent over so no one could see my face as I clenched my teeth and tried to talk myself through it.

Not now! There's no time for this now. Breathe, breathe, relax . . . it's easing up. It's going away. Focus on the prize . . . the finish line.

Teammate Matt Wagner came alongside and spoke to me. When I didn't stand up right away, he bent over and asked, "Hey man, you OK?" with a worried tone.

I stood up, flashed a grin and said, "Yeah, yeah, just catching my breath, Matt, I'm cool," trying to be nonchalant in my denial. The words echoed in my head . . . I'm cool, I'm cool. I told myself over and over.

But I still felt the pain, a constant, stabbing sensation somewhere near my waist. I won't let it slow me down. I'll deal with it after the race. Only focus on the race, I told myself, as I reach the starting blocks and waited for the starter's commands.

"Runners, to your marks!"

I backed into the starting blocks, thinking of myself as a piece of spring steel ready to explode. I felt calm as I looked at the finish line and the track stretching out in front of me. Again, I thought of Jim Farmer's 100-yard record, and could picture myself soon breaking it. Everything else was now blocked out, as I began my normal focus finish 15 yards past the line.

"Set" – Listen for the gun and react.

BANG! The best part of my race began after I could get my long legs moving, so my starts were not usually the best. Today was certainly no different in that respect, and as I came out, I stumbled slightly, feeling a sharp pain hit me. No time to think of it now, however, as I had to get moving in order to use my speed to catch those other guys. Focusing on the finish, I was able to put all thoughts of pain and surgery aside while the race was going on. I passed all the runners but one and leaned hard at the tape, sure I had nipped him for first. At first, they called it a tie, but then gave it to the other guy. I was really upset.

But Coach Cockerman seemed suitably pleased with my 9.6 time, even though he still appeared worried. The second place finish did not help my mood. I figured they would have left it a tie, since I had the same time as the winner. At least I still have the 220 coming up, and I wanted to win it to leave no doubt who was fastest. I did manage to win, but the time was slow, and I felt terrible. But at least I had a good start on the season, so I was confident that things would go well from here on out. Little did I know . . .

THE JOY RIDE

Chapter 2

Leading up to the second operation, I was in and out of the hospital for a number of blood tests and radiation treatments. My uncle Chester would try to cheer me up by recalling stories from our days together as kids. When he left, my thoughts drifted back to my early childhood, which had not been the easiest life to live. However, my earliest memories were always of fun things and good times.

I was raised in a predominantly black neighborhood called Bayshore Park in East Palo Alto, California. The "rich" folks lived across the bridge in Palo Alto. My grandparents raised me. They could not read or write. However, they would not allow me to use their own lack of education as an excuse for not doing well in school. They did their best to raise me to be an honest and upstanding young man. In those days, the "spare the rod, spoil the child" theory of parenting ruled, and discipline was sure to follow disobedience. Everyone in our family called my grandfather, Chester Prince, Sr., "Papa" and grandmother Mary was "Mama" also known as

"May-May."

My father lived less than a mile away, and I saw him almost daily. However, he came to visit with Mama and Papa, and we did not interact very much; usually just a grunted "hi" and "bye." None of the men in my father's family were given to outward expressions of feeling for one another, and I really didn't expect more. He and my mother had divorced when I was just a baby, so she was never a part of my life as a child, and didn't come back into my life until after I was in high school. My grandparents rarely spoke of her: Papa, because he would never talk about anyone not in his presence, and Mama because she would naturally take my dad's side. As a result, I knew almost nothing about my mother. I always hoped to find her someday and spent hours thinking of how she might look or where she might be living.

But as far as I was concerned, Mama and Papa were my parents for all practical purposes. As a youngster, I seem to be given to unexpected nosebleeds, and was often "protected" by not being allowed to play with the other children. The grown-ups often treated me like I was very fragile, and I wondered why, my cousins, who were younger, could go to the park or the beach, but I had to stay home. I became a loner, and actually came to enjoy playing by myself in the backyard most of the time. Usually, my cousin Debbie stayed with us as well, and there were even times when cousins Ernest, Johnnie and Robert were there too. We would have a good time playing like typical kids, even though I still preferred being by myself.

One of my fondest memories of my grandfather happened on a Sunday morning in 1959 when I was about five years old. My Aunt Helen (we called her Na–Nann) had just bought a brand spankin' new car. It was a 1959 Pontiac star, chief, salmon-colored, with a long black arrow on the side. Man, I thought that was a pretty car!

Somehow, Papa got the car keys and decided to have a little adventure, using us kids as pawns in his game. We were attending Sunday school at Macedonia Missionary Baptist Church in East Menlo Park. After Sunday school, we were expected to stay for church. But this particular day, Papa was waiting for us when class let out. I guess we should have known that something was not right, but we kids (my cousins, Ernest, 7, his sister, Debbie, 5, Johnnie, 10, and his brother, Robert, 8, and I) were so surprised he came driving up in that car, we just stared.

He shouted, "Hey, kids, hurry up and get in the car!" We were so excited, we were bouncing up and down on the seats, and he yelled at us to quit. Usually we were reasonably well behaved, but this was such an unexpected treat, we just couldn't sit still.

Papa cranked up the car and the first thing he did was run up on the curb. People scattered like flies, trying to get out of the way. This was too funny, and as kids we just couldn't contain ourselves. Most of us had figured out, we were part of a little mischief. We squealed with laughter as people were running everywhere. Sweat started popping out on Papa's forehead. He turned around a bit panicky and told us we'd better behave. We were overjoyed because we weren't going to the 11 o'clock church service.

Papa had brought joy riding to a new level. This was about a mile and a half from our house at 1219 Jervis Avenue. When we drove up, my grandmother and my three aunts were waiting. Aunt Beulah (mother of Robert and Johnny) and Aunt Ruby (Ernest and Debbie's mother) were almost hysterical, worrying about us kids. Na-Nann was beside herself, more angry than worried, since it was HER car! However, the neighbors, the McGills and the Roundtrees, saw it in a different light, as the laughter almost brought them to tears.

We kids didn't know it, but Papa didn't have a driver's license. In fact, he had not driven a car in more than ten years. To make matters worse, since he was only about 5'6" he had trouble seeing over the steering wheel. Na-Nann was fuming when she stepped out to the car and asked, "Papa, why in the world did you take this car?" Papa look like the cat that swallowed the canary as he got out of the car in silence. As soon as we kids piled out of the car, the women started in on us.

"You kids should have known better than to get in that car. Why did you do it?"

We replied in unison, "Because he told us to get in."

We all began to march inside, and as we sat down Na-nann started in again.

"Papa, tell me why you did it!

Papa reached to the back of his head as though thinking about it. As he rubbed the back of his head, he replied, "I just wanted to take it for a spin and see what it could do." Then roughly he added, "It don't ride like no Buick!"

As far as he was concerned, a Buick was the best car ever made. He had never owned anything but a Buick. At this last comment, my aunts just looked at one another, staring in disbelief. Na-nann rolled her eyes and sighed, shaking her head, and said, "Lord, I'm going to have to hide these car keys!" And then the three sisters stared at one another again, as if they had all come to the same conclusion, at the same time, knowing further conversation would be futile. As one, they rose and proceeded to the kitchen. In silence, they ate a few scraps of bacon left over as they reflected on Papa the Impossible!

THE FRONT

Chapter 3

There was a small group of stores on the corner. We often referred to as "The Front." Mama often sent me to the grocery store in "The Front" to buy a small item or two. She didn't trust me to carry the money in my hand for fear I'd lose it, so she would put it in a handkerchief pinned to my shirt.

One day she sent me to the store just to get change for a $5 bill. The storekeeper said he wouldn't give me change unless I bought something, so I went home to report to Mama. Back up the street I went, this time to purchase a box of Morton salt. Evidently my going back and forth had attracted the attention of some bum or drug addict on the street, because when I started home with the $4.85 dutifully pinned to my shirt and the box of Morton salt in a paper bag, a guy suddenly jumped out from the side and grabbed me. The first thing he did was try to grab the money and run, but it was pinned too tightly so he pointed a gun to my head and told me to give him the money. He had his hand on top of my head to try to hold me still. But I knew Mama well enough to know that I'd better not return home without the change – no matter what! To me, the guy with the gun was not as great threat as Mama not getting her change.

So I fought back.

It really wasn't a very hard decision on my part, either, as I started kicking at his shins as hard as I could. It was probably pretty funny to watch him trying to hold the top of my head with one hand, keep the gun in the other, all the while, doing a jitterbug trying to dodge my feet. Needless to say, his hand slipped off the top of my head and I went flying down Newbridge Street for home.

During those first five years, I had fun playing with my cousins and certainly thought of myself as normal in almost every respect. However, I did enjoy the many times of just being by myself as well, and could entertain myself for hours with "make believe." Since I grew up to be somewhat of a loner, maybe that was just part of my personality, even as a small child. I knew that I was slow and methodical. Many times the grown-ups would playfully tease me about my slow speech, and it would frustrate me when they kept insisting that I repeat whatever it was. Sometimes I didn't catch onto things as fast as the other kids, either, and was always more comfortable with a set routine in whatever I did. I did not consider myself an unhappy child, and really didn't recognize my limitations, as being a handicap.

All that ended when I entered the big, unhappy world of school.

TINKER TOY CLOSET

Chapter 4

I have memories of my first day at Kavanaugh Elementary and Green Oaks Junior High School as if it were yesterday. I can hear my grandmother saying, "It's 11:30. We better be going to school." I was dawdling a bit and Mama was getting impatient. So she said, "Christmas . . . all right, Christmas, it's time to go." She used the name playfully. The joke was that Christmas is slow in coming and only shows up once a year. It was a nice fall day, but the trek to school seemed like the longest walk of my life. I wanted to stay home with Papa and watch Perry Mason and Queen for a Day. The change in my routine was already beginning to upset me.

In Kindergarten, socializing with the other kids was difficult because I was used to playing in the backyard by myself. I was shy and my speech pattern was slow, making catching on to the simplest of lessons really hard for me. When the teacher was doing rollcall, she asked for Joseph Prince. I didn't know who that was because I had never been called Joseph . . . ever! I was Dee-Dee (which stood for Dilly Dally because everything I attempted to do was slow and methodical, including my speech). She told me I was Joseph, and when she called "Joseph", I had to answer. Probably unintentionally, the teacher often made me feel like I was different from the other kids. When I stood in the circle, I didn't sing "The Farmer in the Dell" because if I didn't do it right, or fast enough to suit the teacher, I got into trouble. So I would just sit there and stare. That's when I just started disappearing inside myself. I was still thinking things in my head, but I didn't talk to the other kids and I didn't talk to the teacher. That way, I figured I would never get into trouble again. Even when Nap Time came it was hard because I would spend the time with my blanket, rocking back and forth. This soon started to agitate some of the other kids, and so to solve the problem I was exiled to a little closet where the teacher kept the tinker toys and blocks. This was meant to be a timeout, but for me it was an escape into my own little world. I was away from everybody and I was happy and safe.

THE DOOR
EMOTIONAL MELTDOWN

———◆———

Chapter 5

Two incidents with a two-month span stand out in my memory, and tell a great deal about my later actions and attitudes. For me, family had always been those around me, Mama, Papa, my aunts and uncles on occasion, and my father on his many visits. I knew there was another "family" out there, but I had no way of knowing them. My father's family seem to avoid any talk of my mother, so there must've been more than a little animosity between them. Of course, I knew nothing of any bad feelings between them, so I didn't know that I wasn't supposed to like anyone from that side.

I was soon to find out.

I was about eight years old when my mother's mother, with my Aunt Ollie, her husband, Herbert and they're two children, Ronnie, 8, and Gregory, 6, came by to visit me. They had come from Los Angeles, and we're going on vacation and just dropped in unexpectedly. Mama had called me into the living room.

"Dee–Dee, come in here and meet your mother's mother." I was sure that I heard her say, "your mother," which excited me almost be beyond imagination.

Being a bit slow and methodical in my thinking, often caused me not to hear and comprehend the whole message in situations like that. I got so excited that I didn't hear "mother" twice, so thought I was going to see my mother and grandmother at the same time.

Then my Aunt Ollie said, "No, honey, not your mother, but your grandmother and your mother's sister."

When I heard that, I guess I hit an all-time low. My emotions went from ecstasy to deep depression in a split second. It had always been hard for me to keep from showing my emotions on my face, so as a child it was always very apparent what I was thinking or feeling. I was so crushed I couldn't disguise the sadness; just like I first couldn't disguise the joy. I guess I had already displayed too much joy, so things were about to boil over with my family. They would have been happy to toss grandmother, aunt and all into the street if they could have found a nice way to do it. I could tell I was in trouble by the way people were staring at me. That caused my emotional roller coaster to really intensify. I sensed that I was wrong, wrong, wrong, but really didn't understand why. The attitudes made it clear: "you are in big trouble when these intruders get out of here and go wherever they are going!"

Man, I could just feel the tension in the room. It was so thick you could have cut it with a knife. I remember thinking why did these people come here to bring this trouble on me? I tried to pretend that everything was going to be all right, but inside everything was slowly going on. I felt like I was in a time warp or something, with everything out of whack.

My Aunt Ollie seem to have no clue what was happening. She was just having the time of her life. All I heard was "JoJo" this "JoJo" that – and "JoJo, I wish I had a picture of your mother with me so I could show it to you."

I looked around the room, with my head down, and my eyes lowered. Members of my family looked back at me the same way. I didn't know how not to be happy and I didn't know how not to be sad. All I knew at age 8 was that the more I was "JoJo-ed" and the more they talked about me coming to see them in the summer, the more trouble was coming my way later. By now I felt like I was in the Twilight Zone – and most definitely one step beyond anything I tried to comprehend in school.

Now my mind was in a fog, so when we heard the "ding-ding" outside I didn't know whether it was the ice cream truck or the donut truck. My Aunt Ollie gave me some money to go buy a treat for us kids, so with relief, I led my cousins out to stop the truck and buy something. Even outside, my mind was still in a fog. As a result, I didn't see the car speeding down the street.

On any normal day, I would've been the first to notice the shiny new red Thunderbird, but this was not an ordinary day! The car just missed me as it came to a screeching stop. You could smell the tires burning because it was going so fast through this residential area. I was miserable as I thought to myself when these people leave here this incident is going to add one more bad mark to my already long list. I knew in my heart I was finished. I had already felt the discipline that was standard in the Prince family, so even at eight years old, I knew what was coming. I would have liked for time to stand still – frozen, no tomorrow, no lunch, no, nothing. I even caught myself wishing my grandmother and aunt could stay forever in order to put it off just a bit longer. To me any excuse would do, but I guess that was asking too much.

Suddenly, my aunt and her family were leaving, and I could feel the foundation shifting under my house of cards. And yes, just as I predicted in my eight–year–old mind, as soon as the door closed, voices were raised. In my direction.

"Why did you almost get hit by that car? I guess you was trying to show off. I'm gonna give you something to show off about." Uh oh.

Mama continued, "You got nerve to try to look sad when you found out that wasn't your old no-good mother. Like you ain't happy here – all we've done for you. She didn't want you and you got the nerve to call yourself happy to see them? Then you're trying to get more attention by almost getting hit by that car. People will think you are crazy!"

I didn't understand why I was going to be punished for acting happy to see my mother's sister and my other grandmother. I really can't describe much of the next few minutes until I remember seeing the bright specs of red on the wall. As I wiped my running nose, I realized the red spots on the wall were blood. The question just seem to hang in the back of my mind "Why? Why me? What did I do?" Then, mercifully, it was over. However, the question "why?" still stuck in my mind.

As if that were not enough, just too short months later, I experienced the same type of harsh discipline by yet another member of the family.

Even though I was in third grade, I still didn't know my ABC's, so I was made to recite them over and over. It seemed to take me two or three times longer than the other kids to learn anything, so people thought I was trying to be bad by just taking my time. No one seem to recognize my learning problems. I really wanted so much to please everyone that I worked especially hard to learn the alphabet. It was so frustrating because those letters just wouldn't stay with me. In spite of all my best efforts, I got a bad report card. After trying, so hard, and still coming nowhere close to their expectations, something inside snapped. Like the boxer, I just tossed the towel into the ring. I didn't care anymore, so I just gave up.

Now here I was being drilled on learning my ABC's at home. Of course I still couldn't remember them so it must have appeared that I was not really trying. When that happened, I guess the frustration built up too much, because I went through the same bloody discipline experience as before, or perhaps worse. Numbly, I could hear my uncle Chester's voice.

"Stop, stop, leave him alone!" Chester demanded. I'm sure as I look back that he intervened at just the right time, and actually saved me from much more. As I leaned against the door, I felt like it was the only thing holding me up. Then as abruptly as it had begun, it stopped. Through my sobs and tears, I found myself promising over and over, that I would learn my ABC's, even though I knew I had always tried as hard as possible to remember them. In my child's mind, I can make no sense out of receiving that kind of discipline for something I was working so hard to understand. I think I just mentally walked through that door and closed it to everything else. At that point, something inside me just seemed to snap. It was apparent to me that I couldn't meet the grown-ups' standards so I took back the white flag and changed it to a giant banner.

It was like I just imploded. I decided these would be the last words I would speak. If I spoke again, it would be on my terms, and when I want it. You could beat me. You can call me names. It really didn't matter to me. What else could you do to me? if Chester hadn't intervened at that moment, only God knows what would've happened. But at that point, I really didn't care anymore.

Looking back now, I realize some of the thinking behind those awful times. Their philosophy was "whip him into shape so that he can succeed." There were probably some mixed emotions because I was getting a chance for some education. My grandparents never had an opportunity for an education and I must have represented another reminder of their "inadequacy." Perhaps they thought I was just being lazy at times. And had I not been hampered by the learning disabilities I seemed to have, their philosophy might have worked quite well. In any case, I know they meant well, even though my perceptions of their attitudes were so confusing at the time. But since I didn't understand any of this then, my only defense was to retreat into my private world, where it was safer.

Remember, I had decided from this point on, any communication with ME would be on MY terms. So I didn't talk – at all – for more than two months.

Of course, this caused more than a little concern in the family, so I was scheduled to spend time in a few "visits" with the "nice man on the hill." (Read: Psychiatrist) My father would load me up, and away we'd go. Supposedly, I would just open up and talk to this man, but who was he? The only thing he had to offer that was at all worthwhile was the Tootsie-Pops … which I more than willingly accepted. Well, I'm not sure how many sessions I was scheduled to compete with the man on the hill, but the only thing that I remembered at the time was the strange feeling of riding with my father. I don't think I had ever been alone riding in the car with him. After about the second session, I could tell that my father was embarrassed, and all the efforts were just a waste of time. And he was right, because of course I didn't talk for this man either. With no cooperation from me, he decided going to a psychiatrist was a waste of time.

The only thing good about the hill was those Tootsie-Pops, which promptly went to the "candy–store" pocket. Our visits finally ended abruptly when, after another frustrating session, my father's decided to get in on the act. On the way home as we passed through Redwood City, he tried his own small bribe of a stick of Juicy Fruit. In silence, I took it, and promptly put it in the same pocket with my other goodies.

I continued my "silent treatment" for some time at home, and at school. Their inability to communicate with me led the administrators to conclude that I could not function on the regular school day, which was what had led to my half–day sessions. There was talk of "mental retardation" but my stepmother rejected that idea. Then they mentioned having some "symptoms of autism," such as tactilely defensive, opposition to change, avoiding eye-contact, and repetitive motions. Vivian agreed with that diagnosis.

I have since read quite a bit about "Autism" and much of what is described there seems close to what I experienced, so perhaps that was it. My condition is now diagnosed as ASD Level 1. The question remains, however, was my condition clinical or environmental? I was deemed to "display autistic–like tendencies" in the third grade, but it seems obvious to me that much of what I went through could have been lessened with a better understanding of my mind-set.

* * *

And then, my return to the "real world" was as abrupt and startling to my family as my departure from their world had been. Here's how it happened: my dad and his wife, Vivian, (grandmother called her "Doll" because she was so beautiful), decided to buy a bigger house, only a mile from Menlo Park, so I could join them and my sister, Charlene. I remember the first time I laid eyes on Vivian. I thought she had a perfect smile and she brought beauty, grace, and kindness into my life. Most everyone called her Aunt Vivian, so that was how I knew her too. I guess they wanted to help me to adjust to a more normal family lifestyle after that period of silence in my life. Even though I did not actually move in with them, I was able to spend more time with Dad and Vivian, and came to enjoy the experience. She was always very patient with me and I started to grow more confident.

One day, after pondering this in my mind for several weeks, I popped the big question. "Aunt Vivian, can I call you Mom?" I asked. She looked so startled, that I was afraid she was going to scold me, or say, "no," but she just smiled and said, "I was hoping that we would get to this point someday."

I was elated, but still wasn't ready to be hugged. She never forced the issue. It really took me about a year to get comfortable with the word, Mom, because Mama belonged to my grandmother, and the two terms were so close as to be confusing. So one week it was "Mom" and the next it was "Aunt Vivian." I finally settled in with using the word Mom. And I was back to talking.

Although Dad and Mom had picked a bigger house, right across the street from Belle Haven school, Mama decided I would not move in with them. She had raised me from a toddler, and probably knew me better than anyone else. I think she knew how troublesome a move of any kind would be for me. Any change in routine was usually a very traumatic ordeal. Mama's reasoning was that it was a little late in the game for me to be moving "across town" (one mile!) and changing schools. And when Mama made up her mind, there was no use talking about it. She did make the concession of allowing me to stay over there on weekends, but even that was short-lived. My grandmother said that I acted "too different" when I returned back home, and Papa never commented on the situation either way, but his silence was to be interpreted as agreement. I went onto finish the third grade on the half–day schedule, and was considered for retention, but they decided against it, perhaps feeling that things couldn't change much in other case.

So I began fourth grade with a new teacher, Mr. Perkins. I remember him with mixed emotions, not at all sure that I liked what I saw (I still hate black wing–tips), but I'm happy that he tried to help me learn new words and other things. One day he helped me to learn three new words from a glossary in the back of a book. I was so proud that I had learned these three-syllable words I could hardly wait to get home. I wanted to show Mama that I had learned some really big words and I suppose my excitement made it seem like I was "showing off" again. And showing off ALWAYS got me in trouble! Even though I got scolded again, I could see for the first time Mama was sorry for snapping at me. But I had learned my lesson, and never tried to show off any schoolwork at home again.

Even now, as I reflect back on that often–misunderstood child, I'm amazed that this was the same young man who later served for nearly a semester as acting principal at Eloy Junior High School in Arizona.

Mrs. Smith, my fifth grade teacher, was the first black teacher I've ever seen. I was in love with her from the moment I saw her. My eyes were glued to her every move. She was tall and slender, with beautiful features and thick, black hair. I couldn't help but notice her coco-colored legs through the cinnamon-colored stockings she wore. I think she was about 30 years old, 5'9" and about 125 pounds. Anyway, I thought she was beautiful and I use to beg her to let me stay after school on Fridays to clean off the chalkboard.

Then she would say, "Joseph, thank you so very, very much. You stay out of trouble this weekend, you hear me?" Then she would give me an envelope with ten cents in it. She was the first teacher I really liked. I could never find anything bad to say about Mrs. Smith. I wish I could report I learned a great deal during that year, but I really can't say it, since my time was much more occupied within admiring this lovely lady. At least I must've done okay, because I spent the whole year without once getting in trouble. Well, at least not SERIOUS trouble, since I did have to stay after school a couple of times. I think that I got into trouble on PURPOSE those times, because I certainly didn't mind staying after school for her. That was no punishment at all!

My sixth grade teacher, Mrs. Haman, was a totally different story. It was back to trouble city for Dee-Dee. Mrs. Haman was like a drill sergeant. Her attitude always made me feel unwanted, and seem to tell me, "I've got my education … I don't care if you don't get yours, 'cause I got mine."

We seemed to be mutually frustrated and angry at each other, me because I did things slowly and methodically, she because that didn't fit her disciplined attitude. On our way to lunch, we always lined up and marched in close order like good soldiers. And, of course, I was not very good at the close thing, because that meant too many people infringing into my "space." That would confuse me and cause me to get out of step, so one day, she "solved" the problem by kicking me in the back. My cousin Cleve even witnessed these incidents when he was in third grade during recess. It affected him to watch that and he still talks about it today.

She always seem to have a trumped up charge of some sort in order to send me to the office to see either the principal, Mr. Garber, or more often the vice principal, Mr. Patterson. He seemed to be the perfect counterpart to Mrs. Haman, and appeared to take great joy in mistreating people. I sat in his office so often that I became quite familiar with its green marble walls. They reminded me of Perry Mason and the courthouse scenes. On the wall of Patterson's office was a long paddle with holes in it. This was the paddle he used on troublemakers. I assume the picture on his desk was his wife with a big beehive hairdo and black framed cat-eye glasses. I thought they were a perfect couple, with her sitting there just to follow my every move with those cat eyes. She could spy on me, even when he wasn't there, and I didn't dare stand too close to that desk with those eyes looking at me. I never enjoyed my visits with him. I tried hard to keep them to a minimum, but wasn't always successful. Believe me, I was one happy camper when it was time to move on from elementary school. How could it be worse?

HE WORE A CROWN

Chapter 6

I began to look forward to the day when I might add my name to this list of legends – legends if only in my mind, and heroes for a moment in time. It's always difficult for me to truly express in words the feeling I have when I look back on this exceptional group of athletes. In every way, they have become a part of me. Somehow I felt like I was one of them, and their athletic spirit was making a strong impression on my young mind. This was when I first became interested in sports, and I am sure that their positive influence probably served as motivation to keep me away from the many temptations so many of my friends would later fall prey to.

Chester was the Homecoming King of the 1961–62 football season. I remember his black leather-bound yearbook that had ARGONAUT '62 printed in big letters on the cover. I would spend hours trying to teach myself to read this yearbook and pester Chet with my many questions. I would try to remember the faces in the book and memorize the names. In those days all the graduation pictures had the beautiful girls dressed alike in black dresses and wearing a dainty pearl necklace. The guys were also dressed alike in white tuxedos along with all the other fancy things and topped off with a black bowtie. I thought it was so cool. I must admit Chester and his classmates, and all they represented became great teachers and motivators for me in those next few years. The memory of how special he was to me caused me to write a poem sometime later as I tried to find a way of expressing how I felt. My title for it is "He Wore A Crown."

HE WORE A CROWN
It was a page inside a black-covered book.
He wore a crown
Not just any crown, but a crown for a season;
A very special season.
The season was '61–'62 and he wore #62;
Proudly and boldly, that #62.
And he thought he was just playing a game,
That game called football.
I opened that book of '62 and turned to a page.
Again, again, and over again.
On that night, my life was forever changed,
Because he wore a crown.
I knew that I would strive, too,
To be someone special,
He wore a crown.

BLACK PANTHER
LIBERATION SCHOOL

Chapter 7

As the years of elementary school slowly passed, I began to be excited by the thought of moving on. Just the thought of going on to junior high became a great motivator. I would be out of the bad old, elementary school, and only one step away from senior high, and all my heroes. It would also be my first opportunity to participate in organized sports. It is easy to see why I was so excited when the time to start junior high finally arrived, I was ready for a change!

This brings us to Ms. Ola May and her boyfriend (affectionately referred to as "Mr. Corrupt" by my grandfather) who were neighbors across the street. Ms. Ola May was resplendently beautiful and Mr. Corrupt was tall, dark, outgoing, wore super thick lenses, squared glasses with dark brown plastic frames. The glasses were so thick they always appear to be fogged, but he was cool and also sported a cool looking goatee.

Like clockwork, I would serve my weekly after school Tuesday routine task of mowing the front lawn and pulling weeds out of the flowerbeds. This would allow me to stray from the house padding my pockets with some spending change.

Though my grandfather called him Mr. Corrupt (and I called him Morris, his real name) this name was actually complimentary in a backhanded way. Ms. Ola May and Mr. Corrupt exemplified the awakening Black thought of the times. To my strait-laced grandparents, Ms. Ola May and Mr. Corrupt were both refreshing and threatening at the same time. But it must have been more refreshing than threatening, otherwise they've never let me go with him into the big city.

The connection with this young couple and their different, modern views of the world proved to be instrumental in my growth. They both were from nearby Oakland and made frequent visits to see friends and family. They were always promoting a positive self-image, spending a good deal of time lifting myself self-esteem during these trips to the inner city.

Papa was reluctant to give permission for these trips, but I believe on the inside, he thought that perhaps the world was changing for young Blacks in America, and it was better to acknowledge the future than hide from it.

So now I had a new extended family, with a new set of grandmas and grandpas who saw my potential to learn in a whole new light.

Many people will remember the mid late 1960's as a time of protests of the war in Asia and San Francisco and the Bay Area was known for the Hippie movement and the Haight-Ashbury district. Most people remember the seaport city of Oakland and a few of its surrounding communities as a hotbed of social unrest and Civil Rights protests, as well as having the negative presence of the Black Panther Party for Self-Defense.

My sentiments are completely different. I have nothing but pleasant memories. I can attribute this to Ms. Ola May and Mr. Corrupt for allowing me to be myself and never try to push me out of my comfort zone. Their fortitude of vision to try a different approach to my education, though unconventional, gave me a sense of self-worth that I had never experienced before. These weekend surrogate parents were like a warm security blanket, allowing me to experience the outside world like I never had before. What a bonus for pulling a few weeds and cleaning up flowerbeds. I even got a free lunch and take home bag.

Similar "copy–cat" programs sprung up all over the Bay Area. Every community had its own version, and ours in East Palo Alto was called "Saturday Day School." One of the teachers who worked with me, was Mrs. Gertrude Wilkes, who had already begun a program, called "Mothers for Equal Education" which I believe is still working in the area today. Looking back now I realize that for me, especially after the dark days spent in elementary school, it truly became "Liberation Saturday."

At the time, all I knew was that free breakfast programs began springing up all over the Bay Area. I began to hear messages like "free your mind from oppression. Education gives you power." I remember big giant grocery bags with a picture of a black panther – you felt like that powerful cat was leaping out at you. The words on the bag were "Free Breakfast: People's Free Food Program". My favorite phrase of expression soon became, "Right on! Right on!"

So my friends and I started going to the Saturday morning programs for the free food. But I got a lot more than food out of it. Yes, they would feed us, but there were teachers there too who worked with non-stop energy. Even though Saturday Day School was only a few hours long, it was very intense and the level of instruction and caring was deep. I think I was hungry for the positive attention and learning.

Even with the intensity of the classes, the teachers still managed to be patient and were able to bring concepts down to the simplest form for slow learners like me. It didn't seem to bother anybody that I was slow at reading and had to struggle over lessons. The teacher went over each word with me and showed me how to pronounce vowels, and how to figure out the words phonetically. Each Saturday, I looked forward to another lesson and slowly I was learning to read better. It seem like a big burden lifted off my shoulders, and a whole new world was opening up to me through reading. I never realized what a difference it made to read until I was able to do it. Even Papa got in on the act, at least indirectly. He had begun learning to read only a year or so earlier so as I practiced my reading, he could "help" me and thus get to practice his reading, too. My cousin Cleve often helped me, so both of us became Papa's personal tutors, and we would spend hours working together to read. However, Saturday Day School was not the same as tutoring Papa, and I would do my best to get out of it. It was a whole lot more fun to be out playing, so I used every excuse I could find to get out of it. School is different because I WANTED to be there, and the food was good, too!

The teachers were always cheerful and used a lot of positive reinforcement with regularity, which was quite a change from my elementary school experience. I went to the program for about four to six months. By then I was reading, often still struggling over some words, but at least it was making sense to me. I realized that I was not dumb, despite what many of my elementary teachers had always implied.

East Palo Alto local leaders such as Mrs. Gertrude Wilks and Mrs. Mouton always preached self-esteem. I remember the words, "open up your mind and the knowledge will flow like a river." It was the late 1960's and this was a powerful time for me. Personal growth and better times were on the horizon, but I just didn't know it.

SUPER SUNDAY: PAPA'S BIG DAY

Chapter 8

It was on a second Sunday, Youth Sunday, at the St. John missionary Baptist Church in 1968. This was a morning of great anticipation at the Prince household, even though everybody was trying to act as normal as possible. You could tell that Papa was a bit on the nervous side, but Mama was just being her usual Sunday morning self. She was the organizer, rushing people, making sure everything was in order and ready to get to church on time. My cousin Debbie and I knew better than to even halfway look as if we wanted to take our sweet time, because Mama was not patient on Sunday morning. She always had that look, as if she were daring us to say something just so she could pull an ear off our heads. Even when we appeared to have the attitude, "Don't rush me," we would know it was coming. "THAT'S 'CAUSE I KNOW YOU'RE GONNA ACT UP IN CHURCH, AND IF YOU DO, I'M GONNA PUT SUMPIN' ON YOU AGAIN." Sunday morning we were on our best behavior!

Breakfast was the usual, staple: grits, with bacon from the box of bacon scraps. (Oh, how I loved those scraps, because you could often get some GIANT pieces!) Also included were Mama's homemade biscuits, scrambled eggs, and my favorite, chocolate milk. By the time we had finished breakfast, it was about 9:25 am. Debbie and I had to make our way down to the church because Sunday school started at 9:30 am. It only took us five minutes to make our way down to the church, but we dare not be late, especially today.

Well, we got through Sunday school, but the anticipation was killing both Debbie and me! I was supposed to sing with youth choir that morning, but opted not to, since singing with the choir meant that I would have had to march in with the choir. That in turn meant I would have to miss the devotional service because the choir marched in after the devotional service was finished. The devotional was what all the excitement in the Prince household was about. As usual, Sister Payne began to play the piano while the people were finding their seats; as the music played, I looked over to see if my grandmother had made her way to her usual seat. She always sat with the mothers of the church (the Mothers' board) had their own section. Sure enough, Mama was there, and she looked up just in time to catch my eye. As usual she had to give me that last stare. You know the look that has the words written in it: "I better not look up and catch you chewing gum church because I know how you are." Sure enough, Mary Prince knew me quite well because I had just slipped a stick of Juicy Fruit in my mouth. I closed my mouth and tried hard to remember not to let her see me chew. I was relieved as the music stopped and the youth ushers closed the doors to the vestibule where the stragglers and the youth choir were. Then came the moment the Prince family had been waiting for. Papa Prince made his way to the front of the church and stood next to the collection table by the pulpit. He looked out at the crowd of 150 sitting in the main sanctuary and upstairs in the balcony, the other 40 or so still standing in the vestibule. He then opened his Bible and turned to the book of John, even though I don't remember the exact chapter or verse. However, I do remember the first words uttered from his mouth: these precious words were "Verily, verily, I say unto you . . ." Then Papa was on his way, and the crowd sat spellbound until he wrapped up his message. For me this was Papa's (and my) Super Sunday. I likened this moment to the way a coach would feel with one second left on the clock in the biggest game of his or her life. It was the equivalent of someone kicking a fifty-four yard field goal in the last second to win the game. I listened as Chester Prince Sr. poured out the sweetest words I've ever heard . . . "MAY GOD ADD A BLESSING TO THE READING OF HIS WORD." My throat was choked with emotion as I thought about Uncle Rogers' pastor, Elder Hicks, who had been giving my Papa reading lessons every Tuesday for the past three years. In addition, my time spent learning to read at Liberation Saturday had allowed me to be able to tutor him every day after school. But I had to admit there had been times when I bellyached about it because I wanted to go outside to play basketball with my friend James Gray. As he finished, Papa walked back to his seat slowly but proudly. Unlike today's modern suits, which are permanent press, in those days one had to be very careful to not wrinkle the tail of the suit coat, or ruin the crease of the trousers, so the picture of Papa, still lingers in my mind, as I remember his final act. He flipped his coattail up and tugged at the knees of his favorite pants as he took his seat. You could hear the congregation buzzing. "LORD, I DIDN'T KNOW DEAC COULD READ!" The music began to play as the whispering continued. Then the doors were open to the vestibule, and the youth choir made its way into the main sanctuary. Looking back, I realize that in those precious moments Liberation Saturday had reached more than one generation of the Prince family.

A Pair of Powder Blue Shoes with Nails

Chapter 9

I remember when my Uncle Chester bought my first pair of track shoes during my freshman year. They were light powder blue with four stripes on the sides. They looked so pretty I was afraid to wear them. I asked, "Why do these shoes have nails on the bottom?" The "nails" were spikes, one inch long, designed for running on dirt and cinder tracks. Uncle Chester Broke out laughing uncontrollably and said, "Those aren't nails, dummy! Those are spikes."

That year I made the Class C team. The C team was for the little guys. In those days they had grouped kids according to a combination of their height, weight and age at the beginning of the season, and naturally I was in the lowest group, but I was just having a growth spurt and I literally sprouted overnight. I started the season at 5'5", 103 pounds and at the end of the season I was 5'9" and maybe 135 pounds. My first high school coach was the very popular Buddy Miller, who had been at Ravenswood since the school opened in 1958. Of course, I had no name, I had been cut from the Green Oaks team due to lack of talent but they kept me on reserve, just in case someone got hurt. I wanted to be a sprinter in the worst way, but every time I asked Buddy what he wanted me to do he suggested I try my hand at running long distance. My teammates called me "Flea" due to my lack of size. The name stuck with me the whole year.

My first high school track competition was in an away meet at Saint Francis High School in Los Altos. My first race was the class C 880 yard run (1/2 mile), which had all classes, Varsity, B, and C together in the same race. I was happy that I finished 12th overall, but third in the class C division, which I thought was pretty good. Coach Miller most of the time thought it was pretty good, too. He finally seemed to know I existed. He put his arms around me and said, "Joe, you have real potential as a distance runner." I wasn't sure that I wanted to hear "distance runner", but his words motivated me to work even harder as I went on to break a class C record in the open two-mile run.

Left: Joe at 18 months with his brother Larry and cousin Ronnie in Los Angeles.

Right: Joe during the Tinker Toy years.

JOE PRINCE

Left: Joe's Grandparents, Chester Prince, Sr., and Mary Lessie Prince.

Right: Highly decorated Joe looks to the future.

Left: Joe's first modeling gig with Dan Walker and John (Janos) Wilder.

Right: Joyous first photo. Mom's embrace provides a calming effect.

Left: Joe's first championship race in the 220 yard dash at the District Finals held at San Mateo College in 1970. Winner was Lamont Wiley, Woodside High School.

Right: Cal Poly San Luis Obispo record setting 880 yard relay team in 1974. Clockwise: Clancy Edwards, Joe, Curtis Byrd, Kerry Gold.

Left: Joe winning the 200-meter dash at the 1976 Double Dual Meet at Fresno City College. Competing against Stanford University, Fresno State University, and Fresno City College.

Right: Joe runs the day before his operation, February 1975 (notice the hospital band).

Left: Clancy Edwards, Fraisure Sumpter and Joe in 1974.

Right: Joe graduating from Fresno Pacific College in 1977.

Joe graduates from Fresno Pacific, June 1977.

There is no beating Joe Prince when it comes to comebacks

By Ed Jacoubowsky
Fresno Tribune Staff

Joe Prince (left) of East Palo Alto is on the comeback track after winning his fight with stomach cancer four years ago.

Above: Joe anchors the 4x100 meter relay in 1978 representing the Athletes in Action track club, which is the athletic branch of Campus Crusade for Christ International.

Above: With U.S.A. on his chest, Stan Whittaker of the University of Kansas hands off to Joe in the 4x100 meter relay in 1978 at the Evzena Rosickeho Stadium in Prague, Czech Republic.

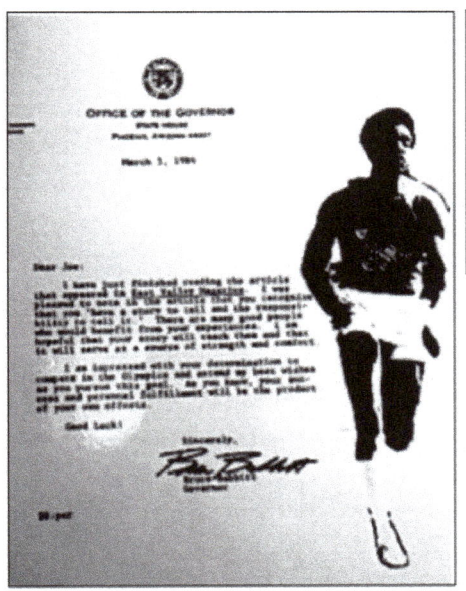

Left: Letter from Arizona Governor Bruce Babbitt in 1984 congratulating Joe on his successes.

Right: Joe Prince, Ron Brown, Bernie Jackson and Dwayne Evans. Going for the Gold article in Phoenix Magazine.

Left: Joe's first speaking engagement.

Right: Joe's daughter, Diamond, at 3 years old in Sahuarita.

Left: Joe at the Liberation Saturday documentary premier at the San Diego Black Film Festival in 2008.

Left: Joe's friend Dave Cole sitting with 3-time Track and Field/Cross Country Olympic Coach Dr. Joe I. Vigil (recipient of the Legend Coach Award from USA Track & Field).

Right: Joe with his co-coaches Jeremy Watson and Alya Verdugo toasting the end of the season at breakfast.

Left: Joe and Mochi discuss solving the world's problems.

Above: In 2012, Joe was awarded 1 of 25 Brooks Sports Nation's Most Inspiring High School Running Coach Awards. He was coaching the Sahuarita High School Mustangs at the time.

SPEEDY CONNECTION TOMMIE SMITH

Chapter 10

Sometimes when someone else believes in you, it forces you to believe in yourself. Tommie Smith was one of the best things that ever happened to me. It has always seemed that God has brought the right person into my life at just the right time, and He certainly did a good job in this case. There are probably few times in life when a young person needs a guiding hand and a mentor more than the sophomore year in high school. Freshmen are too dumb to know how low they are on the high school pecking order. Seniors are top dogs. Juniors have only a short year before becoming top dog themselves. However, it seems sophomores are in between in everything. And at least in my case, I was the most in-between young man you could imagine. My molehills were always mountains, and the more help I could get from a person I respected and admired, the better it would be.

Smith was a world-class champion sprinter. He won a gold medal in the 200 meters at the Mexico City Olympics in 1968. He also was the record-holder in that event. Now, two years later, he was the head track coach at Ravenswood, a predominantly black school. I was in total awe of this man. I had seen him in the Olympics on TV and could hardly believe he was at my school now. Anyway, this same Tommie Smith entered my life at a point when I was trying to find myself. To me he was all courage and honor because he believed in what he did.

It was the last few weeks of February 1970. Tommie Smith was a good friend of our head football coach, Bill Vines, who also was Ravenswood's Athletic Director. Both had been athletes at San Jose State University. Smith was still going through many trials following the worldwide publicity of getting expelled from the Olympics, and certainly needed a job. Their prior relationship at San Jose led Coach Vines to convince Smith to work at Ravenswood and he became a godsend to me in many immeasurable ways. I think the good Lord was really watching over me. I will never forget Mr. Smith passing out the track equipment and shaking each athlete's hands. All I could think of was seeing this man run on TV at the Olympics with the longest, most graceful strides I had ever witnessed. Now this angel of a runner was shaking my hand!

I started off the season as a miler because I had run the one-mile and two-mile events as a freshman. I also threw the shotput and the discus because I figured this would give me the opportunity to run on the Weight Man's Relay. I was only 5'9" and 136 pounds, so I was obviously not a great shot/discus man, but this would give me a chance to prove that I had sprinter's speed. The Weight Man's Relay was always the last event. The people in the stands always got a big kick out of watching Big Jim Lane, who was 6 feet tall and 260 pounds, run with the baton in this 440-yard relay. Each runner ran 110 yards, and the crowd loved to cheer "Big Jim, Big Jim" when he ran the third leg of the relay. I will never forget the day

I ran the anchor leg of that race, being so much smaller than Jim and the other true weight men. When it was my turn to run, I took the baton from Jim and started running. The crowd was cheering and much to my surprise, the announcer yelled, "LOOK AT THAT LITTLE ANCHOR MAN GO!"

After the race, Coach Smith came up to me and said, "You're just like me. You're able to mow people down. I wouldn't be surprised if you're the man to break my world record in the 200 meters."

I was both surprised and proud that Coach Smith had really noticed me. I became a sprinter because I so much believed this man. It was like he saw something in me, some real potential. He could have just been telling me that to make me feel good. But guess what? This kid believed him and that marked a turning point in my athletics. He was no longer just Tommie Smith, the Olympic champion, but MY Coach Smith.

After that meet, he began to call me "Joey Jett" . . . he and assistant football coach Ed Lambert called me by that nickname. The only thing I regretted about the 1970 season was that I didn't start sprinting until almost the end of the year.

I started my sprint career on junior varsity at the S.P.A.L. Championships, where I finished second in the 220-yard dash to Lamont Wiley, from Woodside High. He ran 23.2 and I ran 23.3. I think people were surprised when I placed second. That was only the second time I had run the 220. The first time was a week earlier when I ran 24.0 in the trials and 23.8 in the finals of the district championships. Coach Smith seemed suitably impressed, and I was pleased at the progress I had made.

Our last meet of that season was the Hollister Relays in Hollister, CA, a small town near Salinas. Coach Smith needed a fourth runner for the Varsity 440 relay, which was about ready to begin. He talked first to Percy Puckett who was our fastest junior varsity sprinter. However, Percy had opted to stay down on the J.V. team in order to run the open 100-yard and the 220-yard events. I guess Coach remembered my good 220 that I had run, because next he summoned me. He looked me in the eye and asked, "So, Joey Jett, you really want to be a sprinter?"

"Yes, sir," I replied, wondering if he was joking with me or about to really give me a chance to show my stuff. This could be my moment, my big chance.

"You know, it takes talent to know talent. Do you know that my college coach Bud Winter wrote a book? It's called So You Want to be a Sprinter.

My question to you is, 'Are you up for the challenge?' If you think you can handle it, I'll put you in this relay. You'll run the first leg." My legs were shaking so badly that I just nodded my head up and down, meaning YES. Then I heard the announcer's voice . . . "First Call 440 yard relay" . . . then the 2nd call . . . I had to hurry . . . and then the final call . . . "VARSITY—LAST CALL—VARSITY 440 Yard Relay", it boomed . . . "Ravenswood in Lane Four" and so on.

I was so nervous I had to sit down on the grass to remove my sweat suit bottoms off of my trembling toothpick legs . . . then I was pounding in my starting blocks on the cinder track. My knee was embedded into the reddish colored cinder as I snuggled into the starting blocks. Coach's only advice to me was . . . "Mow 'em down, Joey Jett." I kept hearing that phrase over and over in my mind. Tension mounted and my heart felt like it would jump through my throat. I concentrated on not making a false start and focused on the runners in lanes five and six. This was "make it or break it" time for me - the turning point in my athletic career.

Bang! The gun went off and in less than 40 yards I had made up the stagger on the runners in lanes five and six. I was on them like a police car without warning. I passed the stick to Ernie Spencer, Spencer passed to James Shirley, Shirley passed to Eddie Johnson, and Johnson crossed the tape in victory. Our winning time was 44 seconds flat! We all went crazy, jumping for joy. Thank you Coach Tommie Smith for believing in me!

Later I got a really neat sweat suit from Coach Smith. In those days, the athletes usually chose an athletic company to represent, which would furnish you with all the equipment you needed. He represented the Puma Company, and these were some of their best sweats, a beautiful blue and white outfit. I like to believe that he had worn it in some big meet somewhere, and now it was MINE, so maybe it would make me fast, too. Anything to gain an edge! I treasured the outfit so much that I have taken good care of it over the years. In fact, I still have those sweats, though the elastic is gone from the waistband, the jacket zipper is frozen and won't even move, and the collar is frayed. I still cherish this because of the memories, and most of all I cherish the memory of an Olympic champion sprinter and masterful coach, Tommie Smith. He, more than any other individual in my life, gave me a real goal. He helped me to dream about things I might be capable of accomplishing.

MRS. REAL

---◆◆---

Chapter 11

I enjoyed every day of my high school experience. From the time I was seven years old, I had wanted to go to Ravenswood High School just like Mike Phelan, Doug Wadley, Ray Askew, Nate Branch, Milky Johnson, Milt Dickerson and Gene Tate. Uncle Chester was Homecoming King, Mike played football, Ray was All-League Running Back, Nate, Milky and Milt were basketball stars, and Doug track and field. All I wanted to do was be like them and wear that big "R" on my letterman sweater. I was having success on the track and I started believing I was SOMEBODY. I was beginning to achieve a minimum amount of success in athletics; I guess you could say I got a little big for my britches because I started believing the hype and lost focus by skimming on the homework. I was quickly grounded back to earth by my English teacher, Mrs. Real. She was the real deal! If I didn't turn in an assignment, I was given a chance to make-up, but I figured they would let me slide. I was DeeDee Prince, track star! As I was getting on the activity bus to go to a competition, Mrs. Real was waiting for me. She said, "Listen here, Mr. Hotdog!" It was a swift and humiliating march back to her classroom where I completed the assignment. The saving grace for me was that the clouds opened up and it rained so hard the meet had to be cancelled because it was a dirt track. Mrs. Real didn't care that I had all the medals and could run fast. She wanted me to be accountable and to know there was more to life than just sports. She was going to put me on a short leash, and every time I was late in turning in my homework, the leash was going to get shorter and tighter. I got the message! The lady had authority, but also a lot of love. She was the real deal!

Mrs. Real couldn't always be there to keep her thumb on me but I could always count on my best high school friend Roy Lee Williams, and Mr. Clyde Jeter, Mr. 5 x 5. He was 5'5" tall and 5' wide, the long-time school custodian. He always had a special word of encouragement that kept me on the straight and narrow.

It truly took a village, the dedicated people of Palo Alto, and patience for me to land on my feet.

Academic dean Mr. Doc Cheney helping me with my science projects, my track coach Vernon Thomas, my tutors, Tim Peebles and Tony Simon. Last, but not least, my mind drifts back to my elementary years to two guys who would walk me home on occasion and they're good cop bad cop routine. Wilbert Webster, the Ravenswood varsity 2 mile holder encouraging me to run whenever I had the chance and Willie Windom making sure I knew he was watching my every step, even if I couldn't see him. I could never figure that one out, but it kept me walking in the right direction.

FINDING MY DREAMS

---◆---

Chapter 12

My dream of being like Uncle Chester and his friends seemed to be coming true. The message to me was being an athlete is not who I am; it is what I do. I must remember there is life after athletics; have fun but stay focused.

I had another dream, but I didn't talk about it much. It was to meet my mom and see what she looked like. When I was eighteen months old, my dad convinced my mom to let me come with him for a 2 week Christmas visit. He dropped me off with his parents, and the two weeks turned into a lifetime. Finding my mom was a dream that was always living inside me. As a teenager, I immersed myself in the soulful sounds of the Motown and Stax labels along with other artists who captured my attention: Isaac Hayes, The Whispers, The Chi-Lites, Curtis Mayfield and the Impressions. That music seemed to help me keep my dream alive. The words in their songs kept me holding on to that little string of hope. Words that vibrated freely through my thinking and really reached out to soothe my heart; songs like,

"Keep on Pushing", "It's All Right", "I Need You", and "Moving on Up". In the midst of this storm I was going through, their music seemed to help me keep my dream, alive. Maybe one day I would find my mom and know what she looked like.

In my junior year when track season rolled around, Ravenswood had a new head coach, ex St. Louis Cardinal's Running Back, Roy Shivers. I felt this would be a great year and even looked forward to the hard training. I seemed to thrive on the hard work because it supplied that needed order and discipline in my life. I was on my way to reaching my dream of being like Uncle Chester and his friends.

This year the State meet would take place on the campus of UCLA. LA . . . I knew my mom lived in LA! A plan began forming in my mind. I had to find a way to qualify for the California State meet. It came down to me having to qualify for the CCS (Central Coast Section) where only the top three from the finals would advance to next week's state championship competition. I was really nervous. I just had to get to LA. The track meet was my ticket. At the competition, I ran anchor in the 440 yard relay for Ravenswood. We finished second behind Monterey and ahead of Sunnyvale. I at last was going to LA! I would be close to where I knew my mother lived and another step closer to my dream! My excitement was hard to contain as we left the Oakland International Airport and flew to LA. The search for my mother hopefully would come to an end, if nothing else other than to satisfy my curiosity. Well, now my curiosity was getting the best of me.

Competing at the California State Championship was an awesome accomplishment. No one at Ravenswood had qualified for that meet in five years. By the time athletes got to the CSC, all the pretenders were gone.

The competition was fierce but exhilarating, and we ended up finishing sixth in the preliminaries and setting a school record in the process: 41.9 seconds in the 440 yard relay at the State Championships at UCLA.

Now it was time to move on to the next dream . . . finding my mom. The first thing I did was go through the white pages of the gigantic LA telephone book. Man! My mind started playing tricks on me and my fingers seemed to go numb. Suddenly I couldn't remember the name I had carried around in that secret compartment of my head for almost ten years. Now I'm saying to myself, "Slow down, slow down. Take a deep breath." Suddenly . . . "THAT'S THE NAME!" I picked up the beige telephone. I dialed the number and a woman's voice said, "Hello." I was speechless for a moment. I had finally tracked down my mother! I could hardly believe it! We agreed to meet. The anticipation was killing me so badly that the hours until the next afternoon seemed to take forever. That afternoon was indescribable for me, a roller coaster of emotions, but surely the best day of my life. I spoke first as I stood at the door in disbelief. "Are you really my mother? You're so little!" I had fantasized for so many years that I really wasn't sure WHAT to expect, but I guess I was past being surprised by the whole thing. I spent that night with my mother and my grandmother. We talked and laughed, trying to cram seventeen years into one night.

My mom asked me a simple question. What do I like to do with my spare time? I immediately went into panic mode and couldn't think but had to say something. I rattled off, "My friend, Eric Walker, he's kind of like my little brother, we listen to the radio. We discovered KDIA Lucky 13 AM San Francisco Oakland on your radio dial and KSOI 107.7 FM with Johnny Quick and Hard Punchin' Herrmann Henry. Anything from Leonard Bernstein to Ray Charles to Tower power." I was hoping she was impressed with my conversation.

ST. LOUIS....?

———◆———

Chapter 13

Looking back I hadn't given much thought about college or life after high school. One afternoon my uncle approached me as I was playing basketball in my backyard by myself which was a regular routine for me. "We are going to get you a suitcase. We're going off to college. I've enrolled you in a special agricultural program for young adults from at-risk communities. You will learn to work with your hands." I ran off the names of a few high-powered universities in the area: Stanford, Cal, Berkley, UCLA. He had a shocked sort of look on his face. At times he could be something of a rascal; he just smiled and said, "Nooooo, not quite. You're going to San Luis Obispo." And just like that, in a matter of days we were off to college. I was so excited! I was going to St. Louis . . . I'd see the Arch, and my cousin, George, who had just moved there. Amazingly, after a two hour car ride, we were there! "I had no idea St. Louis was so close to home!" I told my Uncle. That's when he realized that my hearing problem had mixed up San Luis Obispo with St. Louis. He tried not to laugh, but then we both ended up having a good laugh over it. It was a good way to break the tension about going to a new place. I was a college student now . . . ready or not!

I was totally out of my element and out of my comfort zone. I had been sheltered for the most part by my grandparents, teachers and friends. I guess you could say the village all had a hand in raising and protecting me from real world harm. Now I was going to be on my own. These were extremely anxious times that took me far beyond my comfort level. You know that old Southern expression, "Nervous as a long-tail cat in a room full of rocking chairs? Well, the first few months away from home were not the highlight of my young college career.

There were a few people on campus who seemed to realize that I wasn't comfortable in social situations because of my lack of eye contact and being a bit leery of being touched. I guess I was a real easy target to read. They were big city guys, or at least they thought they were, and they seemed to feed off each other. Brushing up against me while we were playing pool, doing whatever they could to make me skittish, I became a source of entertainment to them. After a couple of off-campus incidents at the Stenner Glen Dorms, involving a few tussles and wastebaskets flying across the room, those wanna-be intimidators with smirks on their faces decided it was probably best to give me a break and acted appropriately cautiously from then on in respecting me and my space.

That year did produce two positives; first, I was given an athletic scholarship for track, and second, I met a 17 year-old tailback, Gary Curtis Davis, (future tailback for the Miami Dolphins), an upcoming star player on the football team and high jumper Reynaldo Brown, the youngest member of the 1968 Mexico City Olympic Team. Instantly we had a mutual respect for each other and knew we would always have each other's backs. To this very day, we're still that way!

My Cal Poly track scholarship gave me the opportunity to train with a young coach, a former All-American hurdler, named Steve Simmons. Although he wasn't much older than I was, he had the skills and the patience to deal with a troubled adolescent on the autism spectrum. Although from time to time our relationship was sort of strained, I admired his outgoing personality and secretly wished I could be that way. I wish I had let him in more . . . it wasn't for lack of trying on his part. I have always owned my part of the blame for the estrangement due to my lack of communication skills. What was most important, however, was his coaching skills. He helped me become a conference champion and gain All-American status.

I was ecstatically happy after becoming a conference sprint champion and also earning All-American honors, but the toll of being at Cal Poly, San Luis Obispo, a campus of 15,000 students, and the pace of academics was a bit overwhelming for me. I realized in order for me to find success academically, I was going to have to accept a change in direction.

A LITTLE HELP FROM MY FRIENDS

Chapter 14

My sophomore year of college I enrolled at Fresno Pacific, a private faith-based college with a student body of only 480, this time with a lot of hoopla - Big Man on Campus Scholarship and title of All-American to live up to. The first meet and first weekend of the new season I equaled the second fastest time in the nation. The time did not hold as the season progressed, but at least on that day I held my own with the best of them.

The day after my track debut . . . total implosion! I entered the hospital for removal of a tumor, and the next 2 1/2 years I was in the fight of my life. I was in and out of the big house (hospital), having extensive surgeries and treatments and fighting the "big C". A highlight during this time was a visit from Nate Branch, a hometown hero and friend of the family I'd known all my life. Nate played for the Ravenswood Trojans and University of Nebraska Cornhuskers and was now a member of the Harlem Globetrotters, who were playing a game versus the Generals at

Selland Arena. He stopped by my bedside at the hospital along with the world's most famous dribbler, Curly Neal. It really gave me a boost and put a smile on my face.

During this ordeal, the student body, faculty and staff encouraged me not to give up on my dreams and never lose faith in earning a college degree. On the day before Christmas Eve my junior year, Coach 'Ham reminded me that Pacific wasn't just faith based in name only. They stayed true to their word and honored my scholarship even though I was no longer able to compete. This is my most treasured holiday memory. I also formed a bond with my track teammate who would later become my lifelong primary health care physician, Don "the Bear" Gregory. He was so dedicated to our friendship that he would sleep in the chair in my hospital room at night. Knowing that I loved Benny Goodman, he went out searching for any Big Band records he could find and put them on tape for me so I could listen to them while I was healing. He was determined that I was going to get better and that he was going to become a doctor. It's only fitting that he has become my doctor and is continuing to oversee my healing.

At different points along life's journey, there's going to be suffering which gives you a chance to learn about yourself and those around you. The combination of music and laughter was a great medicine for me. I remember retreating to the music room on the Fresno Pacific campus, banging on the piano for hours banging and hitting all of those wrong notes. A young lady named Janice Hurd, a student from the nearby city of Lemoore, would encourage me to keep playing even though she was busting up in laughter. Her laughter kept me going and she kept reminding me, "Be patient. It will happen. Patience, please!"

A TALE OF TWO BOYS AND A MAN

Chapter 15

Sometimes events occur in a person's life which have an effect lasting far into the future. Two such events occurred to me in a way that seemed to connect them in my mind. Both of them had a profound effect on me, and I remember them with joy. The first one was what I call "A Tale of Two Boys"; the second "A Man."

Two Boys. There are times when I reminisce and ponder on how my life might have turned out differently if it worked for two little Hispanic boys running down MacArthur Street in Redwood City, CA. It was a warm summer evening in 1973.

I was standing on the front porch, visiting with my friend, Sedrica, saying my last goodbyes before I was to leave for college at Cal Poly -San Luis Obispo. I can still remember that moment as if it were yesterday. I was watching two boys (ages about 8 and 11) as they ran under the dim streetlight over a 50-yard stretch of pavement. The older boy threw up his hands is he pretended to cross an imaginary finish line in victory, his eyes looking toward the heavens. The sky was camouflaged and shielded with a touch of quarter moon, and powered stars sprinkled over. I stood there, astonished at what I just heard!

"And Joe Prince wins again!" We looked at each other in amazement. So I called out to the two boys and asked them to repeat what they had just said. Again the eldest boy said, "I said, 'Joe Prince wins again.'" The egotistical part of me wanted to ask the two boys if they knew with whom they were talking. But after looking at the gleam in their eyes as they spoke, I realized the sprinter they knew as Joe Prince had become their hero. This person was bigger than life to them.

The only thing I could think of was that in 1971 and 1972. I had dominated the competition at the Sequoia Union District Championships. The meet took place in Redwood City at Sequoia High School.

My better judgment stepped in and told me to let it go, so as not to spoil the moment. These two boys probably wouldn't believe me anyway. Years later, I realized this was just what the doctor had ordered; God would use this memory to carry me through the hard times to come.

So many restless and painful nights in the hospitals, I realized those spoken words from out of the mouth of babes, "And Joe Prince wins again," had now become bigger than life to me. Thank you for the memories, little ones. I'm glad my ego didn't get the best of me that evening, because I'm sure it would have spoiled the moment and the memory.

The Man. His name was Willie Willingham. I was first made aware of Willie in the summer of 1974 in San Bernardino, CA. My mom, Mildred, had decided to make a rare appearance at Reverend Johnson's church on 9th Street. Going to church on Sundays was not always at the top of Mom's list of priorities due to the lack of financial fortification to drop in the collection plate and a shifty means of transportation to get there. Mom always felt bad if she couldn't walk around and at least contribute one dollar to the plate; in her house George Washington was not the easiest person to find.

Moments after we had taken our seats in church, my mom looked as if she'd seen a ghost as she blurted out, "Dee Dee I know I can't be seeing what I think I'm seeing, that can't be Willie Willingham!" A few seconds had passed by, and Mom impulsively sat at the edge of her chair . . . "That IS Willie Willingham! Make sure that I tell you about him as soon as we get out of here."

I had not spent much time with Mom. We were still trying to get to know each other's ways. This was the first time I've ever seen her spooked. I was trying to figure out what was so mysterious about this tall man singing in the church choir. At first glance you couldn't find anything special about him. I just figured she liked a tall man. He had pitted, dark skin, stood about 6'4" and weighed about 180 pounds. But the more I observed this man's actions as he sang, draped in a maroon colored robe, belting out base notes like I had never heard. I'm saying to myself, "this dude can sing!"

I nudged Mom. "Tell me about that man." She replied, it's too much. I'll tell you after church."

By this time I had marked his every move, his spirit had drawn me in. I was hooked on the joy this tall man had displayed. All I wanted at that point was for church to be over so Mom could tell me about that man.

Well, church let out, and the tall man disappeared. On our way home, Mom began to tell me about the tall man that she had known for a good number of years. She had to pour out his story. At the age of 16, he sang with the Jewels, a rhythm and blues band that had a big hit record, "Hearts Made of Stone." This song had climbed all the way to the top of the charts in California. It also received a lot of regional airplay. As a teen group, the Jewels, with 1950's hit, made way for television shows and endless nightclub engagements. Willie had made the big time. In the mid-60's, he had joined a fast-moving group, The Rollers. Willie was on a roll; the only thing was that he was rolling downhill totally out of control without realizing it. He began to live a lifestyle of drugs and alcohol. He became hooked on more and more pills to get high and a fruitless search for joy and peace. The wine and drugs made him abandon his job and friends. By this time, he had no group to sing with and life had become empty.

Willie wound up on the streets of San Bernardino, CA; he became a drug pusher, hustler, anything to make a buck. The street can be a very cold way of life. Mom spoke of how he had almost died on those unforgiving streets after being knifed in the stomach. She said he was always in and out of jail. The jailhouse had a revolving door for him. The more she revealed of his past, the more I would think about him and wonder how this man with so much joy could remotely live the life she had described.

Every time I called Mom from college, I would ask her if she had seen that man. Sometime she said, "I think he's still at Reverend Johnson's but I'm not sure." Every time I was scheduled to go back into the hospital, I would think of that man and wonder if he was still holding onto his joy, his faith. For some unknown reason, I just couldn't shake the memory of that man. I would think about how Mom talked about him walking the streets of San Bernardino in the 100+degree weather with a filthy dirty wool overcoat, begging for pennies, dimes, nickels, or whatever one could spare just so he can go buy a bottle of cheap wine. This ghost haunted me.

I was burdened with the uncertainties of life and feeling down in the dumps. I guess Mom had noticed that I didn't inquire about that man anymore, wrapped up in my own selfishness. Out of the clear blue, she said, "I'm not sure, but I think I heard that Willie Willingham might be at Loveland."

I replied sarcastically, "What the heck is Loveland? Is it some kind of amusement park?" Mom replied, "Loveland is the church where your brother Gerald has been going in nearby in Fontana. Pastor is Chuck Singleton."

I said, "Let's check it out. He might be at tonight 6 o'clock service."

And so we did. We finally met face to face, but I shall never forget the moment of anticipation as I finally got to say hello. It was almost more than I couldn't endure, as time seemed to stand still at that moment.

After the evening service was over, I made my way over to Willie. He now held the title of Assistant Pastor. I was shocked because my mind I was still thinking of the tall man that was singing in the choir.

Pastor Willingham and I conversed briefly. You could tell that his ministry was in great demand, judging by the line of people waiting to share their love with him. I was happy that he felt compelled to give me an extra moment of his time, if I had the patience to let the crowd die down. I waited for approximately 20 minutes. I figured, "Hey, what's another 20 minutes. I've already waited years."

Pastor Willingham guided me into his office. As he shut the door behind us, he said, "So you say that you have been trying to meet me for years?" Very humbly, I answered, "Yes sir." We both felt a bit awkward at that meeting. Then he said, "Tell me a little bit about yourself, son." So I began to tell him that my mother had pointed him out to me in church on 9th in San Bernardino one Sunday morning and she had acted as if she had seen a ghost.

I told him how she told me to remind her to tell me about his life story. I also told him that it was his spirit and the way he was displaying so much joy that captured my attention. I said the memory of him singing in that choir had carried me through some very hard times as well as good moments. I told him how every time I got in the starting blocks, the memory of his joy, and the story that made his joy so complete was totally mind-bending to me.

Then he began to tell me more about himself, how he felt dirty and cheap before he met Christ and how he had a strong Christian upbringing, but he became disgusted with himself. One day he had to admit to himself that his problems were out of hand and too much for him to fix his own. He cried out to God to take the taste of drugs and alcohol away from him and after that any "desire for getting high" was gone. He said, "That's how I got to that place in my life where joy and peace overflow."

Willie began to tell me how the Lord had worked miracles on his job at the Kaiser hospital in Fontana. How people would take notice of his singing as he scrubbed floors and toilets as a janitor. He felt good being sober and holding a steady job. He told me how he began to witness to the patients, and over the years doors had been opened to him. It was truly a miracle he was now an alcohol and drug counselor at that same hospital.

He was now working a job at required a Master's Degree, but all he had was a high school diploma. Then he walked over to me and prayed for me. At the end of his prayer, he claimed JOHN 16:24; we shook hands firmly and promised to stay in touch with each other. The one thing he didn't tell me was that he was fighting the battle of his life, a battle of cancer. I swore I would keep in touch with him.

I kept tabs on POP (he wanted me to call him that). Then one day I heard that Pop had become paralyzed. The effects of a two-year battle with the illness were taking its toll. In those two years he taught me a lifetime of lessons. Well, Pop's wife, Betty, called to say that he had been asking about me. By this time he really thought he was my father and I was ever so proud to be his son. Our bond was inseparable. I took a flight out that next day. Betty greeted me at the door. She was still in very good spirits despite what she was going through. I poked my head through the door of the room in which he was being comforted.

He looked at me and ordered me over to him. "Give your Dad a hug. How long you plan on staying?" I told him I could only stay two days because I had to go back to work. He was content with my answer. Though he lay there, never once did he even remotely come close to complaining or feeling sad for himself. In these two days, Willie gave me a prescription on how to live life. His faith and perseverance was unshakable. I had never heard of or seen such a transformation from the gutter to the Holy Land.

The moment that I always carry in my heart was the time he sent me to the refrigerator. I guess I was taking too long in the kitchen. He reinforced love for me by saying, "Jo Jo!" I'd answer "Yes, Pop." He replied, "Boy, don't make me have to get on you, taking so long."

Man, I almost melted in pride. I could not believe that God would give me the opportunity to bring him water, and the privilege to rub his weakened feet and legs. A few days later, he went home to be with his Heavenly Father. Over a thousand people came to pay their last respects. Willie still had magnetism, even the bums off the street had respect for him. I can still remember as they walked around in viewing. There was a young man about twenty-five years old with a scraggly beard, dirty, cracked colored pants, torn oil-stained T-shirt that was once white . . . shoes so ragged that you could see his toes in them. Well, that was what Willie would have wanted. No false airs. Just come as you are. His favorite song was "Just a Closer Walk with Thee."

Well, Willie is walking now! And He walks with me, too.

THE WHITE WAGON

---◆---

Chapter 16

Later, I tried to run in another meet against University of Santa Clara. I ran with a hospital band on one wrist and a watch on the other. I won the 200, but paid a dear price. It was nice that I had my own little support section. Mrs. Anne Bolden and all of my friends from the West Fresno community choir came to cheer me on. That made me want to run a really good time, but I must've tried to show off too much, because this race proved to be my undoing. Pride would not allow me to let anyone know that I had over-taxed my body, so I sort of sneaked around and got under the bleachers. I felt like all the life was being snuffed out. Courage had now turned into stupidity. This wasn't a game show or weekly TV series where the hero always comes back. It wasn't a cliffhanger, you know: "stay tuned in for next week." I knew that someone had jerked the rug from under my feet, and I was not going to be able to get back up alone.

Reggie Davis was a former FPC sprinter and was back on campus visiting. After the race, he came looking for me. When he found me sitting under the bleachers shivering, he wrapped me up in a blanket and helped me to my dorm room. The next thing I knew was that the white wagon with red stripes was outside my dorm room to pick me up. They strapped my body down on a small bed with cold steel rods on the side, plugged an oxygen hose or two (who was counting) to my nose and we were off to the big house. I was too out of it to know if the lights were flashing. I was tired of deceiving myself, trying to parade around as a well man. As an athlete, I was nothing more than fraudulent. Cancer and its overpowering of my body and its menacing infection of my mind had reign supreme. I had more surgery next week. The wagon had rescued me from stupidity.

I remember how bitter I had become. I remember three brothers who had come to FPC to speak. Their names were Al Hopson, Al Lewis, and Glandian Carney. Some of my schoolmates asked them to come pray for me because they thought I was dying. So the brothers came to the hospital and asked if they could pray with me. I really didn't want to be bothered with them, but I tried to be nice in my refusal. I guess my true feelings showed, because Al Hopson asked, "You're bitter aren't you?" Sourly, I replied, "Yes." He went on, "You're bitter against God."

I just looked at them. Almost stared at them. My brain was not working too well, but I had suddenly recognized Glandian Carney. It's Mr. Carney from Ravenswood! He had been an English teacher's aide five years earlier. I was under all that sedation, and I still recognized him. It brought some comfort and I revived just a bit. They prayed that God would plant a seed deep in my heart that I might be used to glorify Him. We shook hands and they left.

That while the 1976 Olympic games were going on, I had recovered enough to make a trip to Mendenhall, Mississippi, 31 miles south of Jackson. I did volunteer work with the voice of Calvary ministry for six weeks with the Reverend John Perkins. I had met him in California while we were on the same program doing a speaking engagement at Mount Hermann, a retreat area in the Santa Cruz mountains. At Mendenhall, I worked with Dolphus Weary. What an inspiration this man's life was to me! I know that God did not make a mistake, putting him with me for the summer. I was with a group of college students from various parts of the US, working with underprivileged children in the Mendenhall community. When I got back to Fresno Pacific, they gave me five credit hours toward my degree.

I entered my senior year at FPC feeling full and ready to go. But tests revealed spots, so in November I was scheduled for surgery again. But this time, much to their surprise, they found nothing! No one could believe it, first they thought they had seen spots, and now they found nothing, no cancer! Miracles do happen. This was the best Thanksgiving any 22-year-old could have, especially one who was given 6 to 9 months to live three years earlier.

I was recovering quite well and I got my weight up to 156 pounds. I felt better that I had for quite some time. However, things were not rosy in the classroom. I wish I could get my grades and my physical condition to prove at the same time. Unfortunately, I had flunked math twice already and this was my third try I needed the class graduate and was starting to fill a little panic all of this hard work and now I may not be able to graduate because I can't pass this monster better known as math?

"BIG M"
MARK BARSELEAU

Chapter 17

I got lucky, though, because of Mark Barseleau, one of my teammates. We called him "Big M". Fortunately, he was pretty good at math. Big M was working at a funeral home in Dinuba, which was 41 miles away from Fresno. He'd been picking up bodies and living at the funeral home in order to save money so he could get married. Well, Big M offered to tutor me on my math, but the catch was that I would have to make the 82 mile round-trip when I wanted tutoring. The trip didn't bother me, but the meeting place made me uncomfortable, I felt like I had already been as close as I wanted to be to a funeral home. I tried to get Big M to choose neutral meeting place. I even waved a few dollars in his face, but Big M wouldn't budge. He stuck to a story.

"Brother, I got to be at the funeral home just in case I'm needed to pick up a body. You can understand that can't you?"

I could but I didn't want to. Now I started thinking to myself, this is my last chance to pass math, so I took Big M up on his gracious offer. We met like this the entire spring quarter. I was so determined to graduate that I could even accept being around those bodies if I had to. I wanted more than anything to walk that stage in June. The two months didn't go by as swiftly as I would've liked, but at least Big M got me through.

I passed!

And I even got used to being around the funeral home. He had me guessing people's ages before it was over! I can't say that those tutoring sessions were fun, though. Those twice-a-week sessions help me realize that in order to succeed in life, you may have to make some sacrifices. You can always find a way to survive, if you really want to. Good comes to those who are strong enough to endure.

A week later, psychology professor, Dr. Orrin Berg decided to test me orally on my final make up exam. I had failed the written exam not realizing that I was being tested. He told me right after the test, "Joe, you failed your written exam, but you got a B- minus on the oral test."

Time for graduation!

But at the end of each tutorial session, I couldn't help but reflect back to my childhood friend Eric and I listening to the commercials on radio station KDIA Oakland on Sundays.

"The Jackson Funeral Home located on 1901 Harrison St. is here in Oakland for all of your funeral needs. You may decide to start investing in your eternal future by planning to purchase one of our most peaceful locations. However, in time of need, call us here at the Jackson Funeral

Home. Again at 1901 Harrison St. in Oakland."

Well, I was hoping my time wasn't up. I was trying to be on my best behavior.

I WALKED ACROSS THE STAGE

—◆—

Chapter 18

At last, it was the Graduation ceremony. President Edmund Janzen seemed to rattle off the words "Coom Loudy," (you know "Cum Laude", Magna Cum Laude" and "Summa Cum Laude"), to everyone who was ahead of me. But as I walked across that stage of the amphitheater that evening with friends and family looking on, I received a standing ovation. On this evening I remember thinking to myself that it really doesn't matter if they don't bestow such honors on me because I've already been bestowed with the greatest honor of all: surviving cancer. I vividly remember when President Janzen spoke to me at one of the lowest points during my fight. His inspirational words still resonate: If it is to be, it is up to me. I received a Bachelor of Arts degree in Child Guidance/Physical Education. I had graduated! "Thank You, Lordy!" I had never felt so much alive.

A NEW BEGINNING

Chapter 19

Anew decade, and a new coach at Athletes in Action: Dustin Everman. We called him Dusty. At first glance, he could really impose a bit of intimidation if your mind was weak. Everman had come to California by way of Santa Cruz High School in Eloy, Arizona, where we had done this clinic the year before. Eloy was well known for producing outstanding athletes, including pro football players, such as Art and Benny Malone and baseball's Paul Ray Powell. Through Campus Crusades for Christ, Everman had gotten to know Val Christiansen on the AIA team, and had been the one to invite us to Eloy for the clinic. Little did we know that he was looking us over with the thought of volunteering to be our coach. And little did I know that his connection with Eloy was to be my key to a job teaching and coaching ten years later. God moves in mysterious ways.

Dusty arrived in December 1979, but didn't start with us until January. Maxi Parks have been trying to do the workouts himself to get ready for the

1980 Olympics, as well as coach all the sprinters, so when Everman showed up, Maxi handed him the watch, and said, "You're it!"

We really didn't know what to expect from this ex-police officer turned schoolteacher with the strange baritone wailing voice. I said to myself, "Oh, Lord, Oh Lord" . . . My mind had flashed back to 1967 in junior high school and woodshop/photography class with Mr. Carl Winders. This man was almost a clone! He was just a younger and slightly smaller clone of my favorite teacher. He was bowlegged and walked with a stiff back, which made him look almost like he was sitting in a bucket. He walked real slow, so he never seemed to be in a hurry. He was 6'3", about 195 pounds, and bald. Well, at least MOST of the time he was bald! He'd be bald one day, and the next day he'd wear a mop, a toupee, on his head as camouflage. Yes, Everman was a real character and sometimes he could be a bit of a rascal when it came to workouts. You never knew what was up with the toupee, but you knew this man could coach! This would take the pressure off coaching for Maxi so he could further concentrate on his quest for the gold in the Olympics.

The most memorable times for me that or any other season was the competition at practice. It was more fierce than the meets themselves. I realized that if you could hang in practice with these horses throwing down the leather the way we were doing (or should I say the way Campbell, Brown, Gilbreath, and Parks were doing), you could beat anybody. Every day I worked hard, and most of the time I was hanging tough with them. About mid-season one day our workout was supposed to be a 4x300 meters at Cal State Dominguez Hills. Well, Brown, Parks, and Campbell were loving it. I wasn't sure about Gilbreath. He just didn't seem to be too thrilled at what was taking place on the "oval" (track) that day.

Like a mad man, Brown broke out with a 34-second 300, Campbell matched him with a 34. Parks, not going to be outdone, upped the tempo to 33-and-change. Gilbreath was slow getting to the starting mark, but he blasted at 34-second leg. Then it was my turn, and I ran 34, and I thought, "Hey, no problem, I can run with the big dogs." Then it was round two. Brown 33.0 again and Campbell tried to match him, struggled but came through. Parks was ticked off, he covered the dirt in a time of 32-and-change. I then realized that they were running at MEET PACE, perhaps even record meet pace, the equivalent of 45.0 or better in the 400 meters.

Then I prayed to God, because I wanted my mama; I didn't really care which one, Mary, Mildred, or Vivian. I just wanted mama! Gilbreath took off, but his time had fallen off the pace. I was kind of happy though, just in case I had a bad run. But I could understand Gilbreath's situation, he was a world-class, 100-200 meter man. These others, they were world class 400-meter men. Man, two of them had struck gold in 1976 in Montreal . . . The other a third place finish at the NCAA championships. Well, it was my turn, about 33 and change! YES! I had even beaten Gilbreath's split. Everman comes over to me and tells me to take a two-lap cool down, my program's over. I look at them in amazement. I replied "Why? I can hang; I just beat Wardell Gilbreath's time."

We talked back and forth. He finally got tired of my pleading my case, and walked away, shaking his head, throwing up his arms, flopping like bird wings. "DO WHAT YOU WANT!" He shouts, "Will somebody please talk to this child? He runs two good series and now he's the coach!" He called over to Maxi Parks for help. We called Parks the Controller because he seem to always have everything in his life as well as on the track under control. Parks responded, "I've already tried to talk to him. He's too hardheaded. Besides, you're the coach, so he has to listen to you."

Grumbling about how that doesn't seem to make any difference, he now goes to Benny Brown. Benny could get a laugh out of almost anything so he hollers out playfully, "The brother is from East Palo Alto, Coach. You don't get no tougher than that."

Next, he turns to Steve Campbell and Gilbreath there on the grass, and they're rolling and laughing and holding their sides. Teammate Gordon Peppers, not able to do a workout that day due to a slight hamstring pull, was instigating everything. "I guess if God hadn't made him so fast, he could have probably concentrated on being a stand-up comedian because he kept us in stitches." Well, I guess Coach got the message and just shook his head with a disgusted look on his face. He told me to get to the line with a sardonic smile curled on his lips.

I took off as fast as I could until I got to the 250-meter mark. I had hit a brick wall. I literally crawled in the last 50 meters, and "crawl" is not an understatement! In this case, all I needed was to be wearing a pair of cloth diapers or some Pampers because this baby was through! The brothers were all rolling on the grass and Everman was trying not to give me that I TOLD YOU SO look.

After that happened, practice just continued without me. Gilbreath regained his strength, and I think Parks and Brown dipped under 32 seconds. Campbell was close behind. Yes, the fun was really flying that day and at the end of the day> I realized that Coach Everman knew more about Track and Field than I did. After that day, I not only looked at him as Coach, but he also became a surrogate father to me.

TENT MEETING

$$\text{—⬥◆⬥—}$$

Chapter 20

The summer of 1979 may have been disappointing in the way of being unproductive on the track, but other great things were in store for me. That summer I attended a revival in a big tent on the corner of Rosecrans and Bullis in Compton. I was invited by a young lady friend I had met back in the summer of 1977 when I was vacationing in Denver, Colorado. She was with a group of young people from Oakwood College in Alabama. As they passed by me on the streets far away from my hometown of East Palo Alto - I thought I had recognized one of the guys in that group, and sure enough it was someone from my past. It was a guy by the name of Chris Simon, a guy I went to high school with a ninth grade before he transferred the next year. I had not seen him since then.

So through Chris, I met a young lady, and discovered her name was Sharon Pyburn of Alta Dena, California. We all hung out that summer of 1977 and I kept in touch with her the next couple of years. I guess I had become a little bit sweet on her, but unfortunately (for me) I never let her know it. Well, she invited me to the tent meeting, and the famous singer, Little Richard, was in attendance. I thought it was a bit, unusual, because little Richard was not really known for his gospel music. But he did indeed have a story to tell. The evangelist was of the Seventh Day Adventist church, his name was G.H. Rainey. After the meeting was over, I got the chance to meet Richard. He heard a bit of my story and told me that he was touched by my testimony of coming back from illness and the attempt to make a comeback in the athletic world as well. You should never attend an evangelistic meeting without leaving a little something in the collection plate, so I just naturally gave till it hurt. For some strange reason, I had forgotten and put all of my bus fair in the collection plate. Now I was stuck without bus fare and no ride home.

I was in total shock when Little Richard offered to take me home. I remembered riding back to the Silver Lake District of Los Angeles thinking "Can this really be happening to me? Am I sitting here in Little Richard's beautiful brand new burgundy colored Chrysler Cordoba?" As we talked, we shared stories of triumph over tragedy, and both found that we had stories we must tell. So, even long after the tent meeting had ended, Richard and I walked the streets of Long Beach and Compton, passing out evangelistic tracts. I felt like I got to know him fairly well, and enjoyed his company immensely. He was a totally different person than many have made him out to be.

I also spent lots of time with evangelist G.H. Rainey. During that time, I had my first taste of soy meatloaf. I kept trying to figure out why this meat tasted different than any meat I had ever eaten. Richard really got a kick out of that. They didn't tell me what I was eating until I had finished. Evangelist Rainey was a dynamic speaker as well as a dynamic human being. You owed it to yourself to listen to his words of wisdom.

After spending time with him and his family, I made up my mind that I was ready to be baptized. So that summer I joined the Tamarisk Seventh Day Adventist Church in Compton and got baptized by Pastor Gordon. It was at that time that I moved back to Santa Ana and lost touch with everyone, but I'll never forget the great times we shared. I'll never forget the excitement of Richard sharing his unforgettable scrapbook and the story on how his faith has been tested on a plane trip while flying over Kansas during a terrible rainstorm. He said the plane hit an air pocket and he thought for sure he was going to go down. That was part of the reason for his powerful testimony. One of my best memories was the time he brought me home to my Grandmother Lois's house and sat down to chat with her for a while. I think she told anybody everybody in the Los Angeles area about that meeting.

JOE JUST WANTS A CHANCE

Chapter 21

My move to Arizona was not an easy transition. After camping out with Gary Padgett for a few weeks, I finally moved into my own apartment. My only income was the SSI check I was getting due to the disabilities I had from the illness. I pounded the pavement for months, unsuccessfully trying to find a job. I started going to different employment agencies.

Things hadn't turned around fast enough, though. With no money and no prospect of a job, I wound up sleeping in my car at different grocery store parking lots. Carver spent some time trying to help, but nothing came up, until he developed a possible plan of action. His friend, Sam Lowe, was a writer for the Phoenix Gazette. Perhaps Sam saw the human-interest side of my story and write something about it.

I met Sam and he dug up some old articles on me. We talked for about an hour and a half. The story he wrote was called 'Joe Just Wants A

Chance.' He gave the public an overview of my struggle of trying to find a job and of the challenges I had encountered. At the end of the article he wrote, "He now returns to the streets that have become his home."

Well, it seemed to be just the thing needed, because the story paid off for me. I tried to check with Carver on a weekly basis, so the next time I got in touch with him, he gave me an address to pursue. The First National Bank of Arizona (later to become part of first interstate Bank and now Wells Fargo) had called to see if I might be able to fill one of their positions, so I went to the bank and completed an application. They were able to find a position for me as a cash vault teller, counting money all day long. Perhaps not the best job in the world, but certainly a place to start, and at last I could consider myself a real honest to goodness wage earner! In one way, at least, it was great job. Every day I was a millionaire from 10 AM to 6 PM!

Not long after I began working at the bank, I composed probably the hardest letter I'll ever have to write in my life. I realized that it was dishonest of me to continue to receive the disability checks now that I had a permanent job. The SSI (Supplemental Security Income) checks I have been getting for six years at $375 per month would have to stop. It was scary because that check would become my security blanket, not enough to make me rich, but I could count on it every month. On top of that, I still owed so much money, that I was briefly tempted to try to keep it for just a little while longer. Of course, God would never have let me rest if I had, so I sighed and took up my pen. My heart was beating just a little faster with fear as I wrote to a place in Baltimore, Maryland. In the letter, I said . . .

"This is probably going to be the hardest letter I'll ever have to write. I've been receiving SSI checks for the past six years. I no longer feel that

I am disabled, since I just got a job as a teller with First National Bank of Arizona. Please help me to help myself. I've decided that I am not going to let the government take away my life again. Yes I've been down on my luck, but the best thing you can do for me at this time in my life is to not send me any more checks. I hope I'm not being foolish and cutting off my nose to spite my face. If working proves to be too much for me, then I'll have to reconsider SSI benefits at a later date. The struggle to find a job has been greater than the struggle against the cancer, but now I have found a job, so please do your part to help me to help myself.

Sincerely Joe Prince"

Well, I did receive two more checks. I don't know if they took the time to analyze my handwriting or what, but after those two checks, they stopped coming. It had run its course.

Now I was totally on my own. I had to learn to get by on just what I had. I did learn a lot about relying on myself to get things done during that time, so I was still growing. I kept this job with the bank for almost 3 years. I was really surprised myself because of my phobia in dealing with math. Of course, reality told me that I was never going to become a vice president or any of the 50 million titles you can earn working for the bank if you stayed there for 50 years or more. That was true specially for me with my math background! I was very grateful to the bank for helping me break that cycle of dependency, but I knew that it was time to move on.

I now knew I could work at a regular kind of job, so the question was, "onto what?" I didn't know just what I wanted to do with a degree in child guidance, but it was something that I should at least try to use. By this time I had moved in with Greg Moore and Dale Vicker, a student at ASU. Dale was also working for the bank at that time. Dale suggested that because of my degree maybe I should consider working with children at the recreation centers of the Phoenix area. I started putting in applications at the Boys Clubs and at the different school districts. I interviewed and got a job with the Phoenix Union High School District's Desert Valley High School, a school for the educable and trainable mentally retarded, as a teacher's aide. I began in November 1983. It was a new beginning.

The problem was that I wasn't really using my degree. In fact, I was probably doing something that any good mother could have done, like wipe noses and bottoms and clean up messes and many other small, but certainly necessary tasks. Not that I didn't feel useful, because the teachers there were very dedicated and hard-working. I especially remember my supervising teacher, Karen McCarthy, and next-door neighbor, Carol Sullivan, and Karen's co-teacher Mike Fletcher. They did a lot to make me believe in my ability and talents. They were great motivators as well, and never gave up on convincing me to get my teaching certificate in Arizona. It took nearly two years, but their powers of persuasion finally paid off. I began doing the coursework necessary for certification sometime in 1986.

THE RUSSIAN BIBLE

Chapter 22

A month after I began at Desert Valley, I appeared in a TV segment put out by the 700 Club, a national Christian TV show. It aired on December 21. The story was about me trying to come back to the world I knew best, track and field. Things had changed a great deal in the short time I had been away from running and hard training. Now these guys were openly getting paid big dollars. Even a little bit of that would look good in my pocket. This would be my last stand. The only thing that was different about me being out there this time was the fact that boredom had gotten the best of me. And if by some miracle I ran fast again, maybe, just maybe I could dig myself out of this financial hole. I was still trying to pay medical bills.

After watching the segment of the 700 Club, there was a mission program called Operation Blessing. It was designed to help the many kids who could not afford things like wheelchairs, or expensive types of therapy. We had a little girl in our class named Linda, who was in desperate need of a wheelchair and the family had no resources to afford a new one. So I had a bright idea and talked to Karen. I asked her if it would be all right if I tried to get a chair for Linda. She told me to let her run it by Linda's family and she'd get back to me on it. The family was more than grateful for any help they could get. So I called the 700 club in Virginia gave them my name and told them that I had been featured on their show a month earlier, and asked if they knew if I might be able to have someone maybe donate a used chair for one of my students. They gave me a phone number of a person they thought might be able to help me. I called that number and a lady answered the phone.

The lady got very excited and kept on asking me if I was the same Joe Prince that she had seen on television. She said she had prayed that one day God would let us run across each other's path. She also said she would like to meet me one day because she was deeply touched by my not giving up when things had gotten kind of tough. This lady was living in Paradise Valley, Arizona, only 20 miles or so north of Tempe and Mesa. As a result of that call, I got the wheelchair that Linda needed and found a friend too.

For almost two years I had brunch with an elderly lady, Lorraine and her driver, Effie. Both were about 70 years old. Every Saturday or Sunday we had brunch together at a small French restaurant in Scottsdale named the Chez Louis. Most often her main topic of conversation was "Honey, I pray that the Lord will work a miracle in your life so you can make one more trip to Russia so maybe you can bring me back a Russian Bible." She also knew the probability of her getting a Russian Bible smuggled back to the United States was going to be very remote, even if I did get to go back to Europe. During those two years, I still knew very little about this wonderful lady except that her real name was Lorraine Mulberger and that I owed her dearly for the new wheelchair, which probably cost a few thousand dollars.

Since I had started trying to train again for the 1984 Olympics, I was also very grateful for the monthly checks she started giving me to help me with my efforts. It took a good deal of pressure off me. But soon my goal of making an Olympic team had come and gone again. I was too stubborn to really face how impossible it had been all along. I guess I was afraid that if I gave up on the Olympics I would have nothing left to live for. My conviction was that God had given me a fast pair of legs so that I could run for Him and then use that as an opportunity to tell others about what He had done in my life. If I wasn't running, there would be no story. So I kept running, even though now it was more from being bored than because I was thinking of Olympic gold.

Then one day Lorraine said she felt that she could trust me after two years. She began to tell me stories about her family in bits and pieces. One Sunday she asked me if I had ever heard of the Four Horsemen of Notre Dame. When I said I had, she went on to tell me that one of her cousins was one of the Four Horsemen. She told me his name was Don Miller. Even though I said I knew who he was, it really didn't strike any kind of cord with me. I began to feel very foolish for saying I knew him, but was sort of trapped by my deception. I should know who Don Miller is, right? Then she went onto explain, "My Grandfather's name was Fred Miller." Whoa, now I'm really lost because her last name is Mulberger. Finally, when she knew that she had stumped me she told me that she was the granddaughter of the man who founded Miller Beer! Man, I was so glad she hadn't told me that earlier, because maybe she would have thought that I was just meeting with her because of who her grandfather was.

Not long after that I was cleaning out the closet in my room. Suddenly, a box on one of the shelves tipped over and something hit me on the head. I looked on the floor to see what it was. My heart almost leaped through my throat as I stared at a book lying there. Stunned, I tried to keep my composure as I thought to myself, "What are the chances, what are the chances, what are the chances?"

So I opened the book, and sure enough I remember that a Russian Bible was smuggled to me in 1978. A gentleman by the name of John Bedding of the Transworld Radio in Monte Carlo had wanted me to have that Bible. The reason I have forgotten about it is because the red vinyl cover had a big ugly batch of ink on it and it wouldn't come out. It was like that when Mr. Bedding gave it to me. It was not a pretty sight to show off to your friend, so I had just stored it in an old box. Now, with this new discovery, I was beside myself with excitement. I guess I was even getting a little hysterical. I wanted to compare them, so I got my American New Testament and first I started with the book of Mathew and I would pick Chapter and Verse at random, things were matching. Then I go to another book and another verse, and it would match.

About that time, Dale came into the room. "Jay, what's up?" (He called me Jay.) Again, "Jay, what's up?" By this time he acted as if he wanted to slap me upside my head because I was shaking so much. So I told him what was up and had him double check everything that I had checked. Sure enough, they matched. I just couldn't believe it. As I explained to him, "Dale, for the past three years in knowing Lorraine, what has been her whole conversation? Since she's become a Christian in 1957, she longed to have a Russian Bible, and never dawned on me, it never crossed my mind that I had one here all the time! I always said to myself that maybe I would make another trip to Europe as a coach or something. We both rejoiced and I could only shake my head in disbelief as God had placed another miracle in my life!

Right away, I took the Bible to a shop that did binding. I remembered that she said her favorite color was lavender. So I had them put a lavender leather cover on it and had "Lorraine" engraved on the front in gold. When I got the Bible back from the shop, I called her. We talked for a little while even though I knew she hated talking on the phone and that she was suffering with severe back pain. I just had to build up the suspense, because I was so pleased with how God had miraculously provided this Bible. Finally I asked her, "Well, just out of curiosity, just how much is a Russian Bible worth to you?" As if she sensed what was coming, she started to get kind of excited and asked me if I had made one of the teams that would be going to Europe. When I told her that I hadn't, it seemed to deflate her spirits, if only for a moment. Then her voice brightened again as she asked me if I knew of someone who had one to sell. I told her no, but that I knew where one was. Then she got really excited. I asked her how much she thought a Russian Bible would be worth to her.

Her reply was, "Honey, I'd pay $100,000."

I couldn't believe what I just heard! Stunned, I asked, "You'd pay one hundred thousand dollars?"

Then I thought of two people I had met with Athletes in Action. One of them was Marvin Delph, and All-American basketball player out of Arkansas. Marvin had turned down a lucrative amount of money from NBA to stay with AIA. Sometimes we put our nickels together to buy chicken my first year with Athletes In Action. We had long conversations about the money he refused while we were eating our bird at the Pioneer Chicken in Santa Ana. He told me that money isn't always the answer to a man's happiness. The other fellow was Ralph Drollinger, Marvins's teammate on the AIA basketball team. I remembered his story from hearing it told at a halftime of one of their games. This 7'2" giant out of UCLA turned down a lucrative contract with the New Jersey Nets. The media response was overwhelming. All three networks, ABC, NBC and CBS, ran footage over and over. They couldn't believe that someone turned down that amount of money to stay with AIA and play for a $7500 missionary scholarship from Campus Crusade for Christ.

Well, in this case there was no media, but I know I did the right thing. I finally told her that I had the Russian Bible and about the chain of events that made the Bible happen. Even though I knew she was sincere about the $100,000, her money was no good to me. Now I had become like Delph and Drolinger. Yes, just for a moment I thought about all the things I could do with one hundred thousand dollars, but for some reason, I knew that if I had taken her up on her offer, God wouldn't let me have peace about it. I have always believed, and still believe, that my day will come and when it comes I'll be ready to enjoy the fruit of my patience. After I told her that I had the Bible bound in her favorite color and that on our next meeting I would place it her hands, she sobbed over the phone, speechless for almost half an hour.

I thought to myself, "What are the chances that a kid from East Palo Alto would be used to fulfill the dream of someone who is born with a silver spoon in her mouth? Just what are the chances? I felt a lot of love in her sobbing, but it became too much for me. I gently hung up the phone and made good on my promise at our schedule meeting place the Chez Louis.

MR. RUSSUM AND THE GREASED-STAINED PAPER BAG

Chapter 23

My old friend Jay Denton introduced me to Jim Russum, who was the principal of Eloy junior high school, and he was looking for an on-campus suspension teacher. They had just tossed the previous one out on his ear. Mr. Russum set up an appointment the next week. The strange thing was that my good friend, Sam Lowe, had just finished writing his second article on me, called "Princely Visit," detailing how I had turned things around and earned a teaching certificate. It turned out the superintendent of Eloy elementary school district, Mr. Robert Lamb, had just finished reading the article and had made the comment, "This is the kind of person we need in this district." He had no idea I would interview for a job in his office with Mr. Russum a week later. Mr. Russum hired me and joked as he shook my hand on the way out the door. He said that any man who had enough pride to do an interview carrying a giant grease-stained paper bag as a briefcase was going to make it in life as a teacher. The job is yours!

I was riding on a cloud.

The experience I had in on-campus suspension, was a very good one for me. It gave me a chance to see many different people on many different levels, and really helped me to grow better as a teacher. My relationship with Mr. Russum was really exceptional too. He was almost like a father to me, always supporting my decisions. We seldom had a situation in which the parents would need to be called, but if it did happen, the parents learned who was the boss. He was just such a fair, no-nonsense person that there was no room for argument.

Mr. Russum was a stand-up guy. He knew that I still had to pass the teacher's proficiency exam. I hold the dubious distinction of having taken the teacher's exam more than anyone else ever. After four failures, they are supposed to convince you to walk away from trying to obtain a teacher's certificate. Fortunately, I had been a teacher's aide in the Phoenix Union high school district and one of the secretarys there, Karen Schmidt, was the wife of Mr. Al Schmidt, the administrator in the Arizona department of education teacher's certificate department. Karen vouched for me and convinced Al to let me keep traying. He said, "You're going to have to pass the test on your own, but you can take it as many times as you need to. Promise me you won't give up." I went from Phoenix (Phoenix College) to Tempe (ASU) to Flagstaff (NAU) to Tucson (UA) and kept making that loop until I finally passed. There are four parts of the exam and I passed them with reading 80%, writing 80%, professional knowledge 80%, math at 92% - can you believe that?! I had told Mr. Russum when I passed the test that I'm going to buy me a briefcase. I finally walked into his office with a briefcase. That big ex-Marine picked me up and tossed me around like a rag doll. He told me, "I always had faith in you! You are now a full-fledged teacher in the state of Arizona. No more greasy paper bags!"

GABE

Chapter 24

So my tenure at Eloy junior high school had come to an end. It left me with strangely mixed emotions. On the one hand, it was very hard to think of losing the ties and all of the memories and saying my Good-byes to the people I cared about. On the other hand, I knew in my heart this melancholy mood would eventually fade. it was a comfort to me as I also realized that change is always a wee bit frightful, but I had faced many changes during the last 20 years. I knew I would face this one as well. Change can take us out of our comfort zone, but who knows what lurks around life's corner? Progress is made through change.

At the end of the last day at Eloy Junior High School, I didn't want to repeat the many good-byes and well-wishing I had already gone through, so I decided to leave a little earlier than the other staff members. As I walked to the parking lot and got closer to my car, I realized it would be easier for me to not look back. I got into my car and fastened my seatbelt. I looked up to adjust the rearview mirror, and noticed five or six arms waving. I was determined not to look, so I backed up slowly and then pulled forward out onto the street. I took a deep breath to relieve the tension and kept repeating to myself, "It's OK, it's going to be OK."

I arrived at the stop sign and turned left onto sunshine Boulevard, as I headed south to Sahuarita. Sahuarita is a small town 25 miles south of Tucson on the way to the US-Mexico border town of Nogales. It owed its existence to the copper mines nearby, but had also become a destination for many retired people.

I interviewed for the Sahuarita position in late May. In the interview, I met with Barbara Smith, who is the Director of Special Services, along with the Assistant Principal Ron Gerhart. I thought I would really be nervous, but I could honestly say I wasn't. However, I was extra cautious about not being too confident either.

Probably the biggest reason my nerves hadn't gotten the best of me was because of my good friend, Larry Cleveland. He was retiring from the Sahuarita School District as teacher and head cross-country and track coach. He had been at Sahuarita and held these positions for over 20 years. I had held similar positions in Eloy for eight years, so we became pretty good friends during that time. I had the utmost respect for him, and his ability as a coach, and often at meets, we talked track or cross country as we shared ideas. Little did I realize he had been noticing and admiring the work I was trying to do at Santa Cruz, so I was surprised when he sent word through his assistant coach, Jerry Price, that he needed to talk to me. I thought it might be some emergency and immediately got back to him. However, he informed me that he was retiring and he would like for me to put my hat in the ring for the coaching position.

Since getting hired as a high school coach always involves finding a "fit" in terms of teaching, we began to discuss what subjects I was qualified to instruct. I told him I held a BA degree in Child Guidance/Physical Education. I went on to inform him that I was also dual certified in Elementary and Special Education. When he heard that, he got all excited because a Special Ed job had just become available at Sahuarita. I looked forward to the day when I might take a regular classroom teaching assignment as well, so I was excited too.

Not that the in-school-suspension job had been bad for me, because I realized that teaching and helping students with their many different subjects had added a lot to my own education as well, but I really did want to give the regular classroom a try, and this seemed like it might be the perfect opportunity. I felt I had many good life experiences, which might help that type of student.

Larry suggested I should call as soon as possible, so I didn't waste any time. I immediately called the District Superintendent, Dr. Donald Wright, and asked him if he would send me an application. He must have sent it out in the afternoon mail, because I had the application in two days. I filled it out carefully and sent it back as soon as possible. It was not long before they called me for an interview. I was ready to interview for what I thought of as my first classroom job. During the first fifteen minutes of the interview, I felt like they were really raking over the coals. Everyone seemed stiff and awkward and it was hard to relax. I tried to keep my answers to a minimum since I did want to appear that I was showing off. At the same time, I did want them to see that I was confident in my ability. The line between cockiness and confidence is a fine one and I was just being extra careful not to step over it.

I guess I must have answered everything satisfactorily, since in time we all seemed to relax a little. Then they asked me to tell them a little bit about myself. I knew I could get to that point; my mind began to drift to think about the possibilities. "Maybe, just maybe" . . . then I snapped too! I told them the reason that I would like to have the opportunity to teach special education was because I myself had been a special education student. "Who could better teach young people with a learning problem than a person who had been told he couldn't learn?"

They interrupted me only a few times to ask questions, and I went on and on. I realized I might be talking too much, so I apologized for taking so much time. They indicated it was no problem, and then asked me if I had any questions that needed answering. I didn't want to look like I was in the twilight zone, so all I could come up with was "How many students attend the school?" They gave me the figures of how many total students, and the ratio of ethnic groups. A red flag went up when they said 60% white, 39%, Hispanic and less than 2% African-American. I wondered to myself if that would be a problem.

However, after thinking of Eloy's largest Hispanic population, I dismissed the thought from my head. As if they were reading my mind, one of them asked if I would feel comfortable working with that ratio. I reminded them that Eloy was also a beautiful bouquet of people.

I took the opportunity to throw in the fact that my cousin, Myra Mayberry, was at the time the national record holder in the 200 meters for Puerto Rico, had run in the Barcelona Olympics, and would be competing in Atlanta that summer. They both stared in silence and I thought they might be confused with my explanation of the relationship. Then I went on, "Oh, she's on my mother's side of the family." That seemed to be the needed explanation, as we all started, nodding our heads and smiling. Then they shook hands with me and I crossed my fingers, hoping they would be calling me soon.

It must not have taken long for them to decide, because the next day, Mrs. Smith called me and congratulated me on being hired for the job. I thanked her, and as I hung with the phone, I was also mentally thanking God for giving me this opportunity. Just a short time later, Superintendent Wright called me and informed me that I was also being hired as head coach of track and cross-country, for the boys' and girls' programs. As I thought about the good news, another idea popped into my head and I wondered to myself, "Uh-oh, did I make a mistake?" Sometimes when things go so well, a negative thought has a way of jumping into your brain. I remembered one of the Eloy teachers telling me I didn't want to go to Sahuarita since the school had not had a black teacher in its 30 year existence. Some of the other teachers agreed, so I thought it would be a good idea to find out for myself. It turned out they were right. The district had classified employees (janitors, bus, drivers, and the like) that were African-American, but never certified teachers, so I asked why. The answer I got was that Tucson has a fairly large black population, and usually takes all of the black teachers. In addition, they didn't seem to like teaching in the rural areas, even though Sahuarita is close to the city.

Rather than let it become a negative, it motivated me even further. Now the job had become even more special. When the teacher commented again about there not being any black teachers, I joked that I guess someone has to be the Jackie Robinson of the Sahuarita Unified School District. In its 100 year history, I'll be the first black certified teacher in Sahuarita history. And there's only one first.

I had until July 1st to sign my contract. The thought of committing myself to new job was still a bit overwhelming, so I hesitated on getting the contract in right away. I still had a few doubts, but nothing I couldn't handle. And then the strangest thing happened. I knew a couple of the boys on the Sahuarita track team, and I kept running into them. I was in Tucson shopping, and they were, Octavio "Tavo" Blanco, and his brother Felix.

"Hey, Coach Prince, are you going to be our coach?" they asked. I told them I was sure thinking about it. I ran into them a couple more times, and I began to think this was God's way of reassuring me. Finally, I just took a deep breath and decided to get it done. I found it only fitting that on the 25th day of June, I was going to turn 42 years old. Mr. Robinson wore number 42. I signed the papers in Dr. Wright's office. I had now become a small part of Sahuarita history.

I felt like I was ready to do some teaching. I could hardly wait. But the funniest part of talking to the Blanco brothers was that Tavo was a senior and wouldn't be around for the next year. I never did coach him, but I had both of the younger brothers, and they were always hard-working and faithful and did their best in their workouts.

Before I knew it, school was ready to start. Upon my arrival at Sahuarita High School for the first meetings, I wasn't really sure what to expect from faculty and staff. But the 11th and 12th grade counselor, Ron Boyter, really came to my rescue in making me feel exceptional by inviting me into his home for barbecue with him and his wife, Pat. Since he was also the head varsity basketball coach at Sahuarita and an avid University of Arizona fan, he later took me to a UA basketball game. Then he and freshman basketball coach Scott Boone talked me into being Scott's assistant coach. That was not a problem for me because coaching basketball has always been my passion. I'm sure it all began as a seven-year-old watching Ravenswood games. I love coaching the game.

To save money, I moved in with Sid Parker, the school's security and groundskeeper. There was a small house on the Sahuarita property, and it only cost a small amount to live there. Sidney really took me under his wing and help me out at times when things seemed to get a little crazy. Big changes have always been a problem for me, and he certainly helped me through the rough spots.

Finally, it was August 16th, the first day of school. It seemed like at least half the students were happy to be back in school, but the other half were complaining loudly that the summer was too short. Dave Holmer, the principal, had prepared me for a problem I might have. Mr. Holmer was a mountain of a man – 6'7" about 230 pounds, and an ex-basketball player. Since I loved basketball that made him special to me, even though his news was not good.

It turned out that Mr. Homer was taking the time to brief me about a particular young man I was scheduled to have in class. I'd never met this person, but I heard so many negative stories about him that I began to wonder if he was some kind of evil superman. I couldn't find anyone among the staff who had anything good to say about him. It looked like they were all too happy to dump this problem on the new teacher. It wouldn't be long before this student will let me know who he was.

His name was Gabe. All I heard was Gabe this and Gabe that. Gabriel W. Bustamante. All he was looking forward to was one or two more years of high school until he was too old to be kept in special education. Then he would be released upon the world with no skills, little education, and not much hope for the future.

Well, Mr. Bustamante was everything and more than advertised. He did not disappoint anyone – he most definitely lived up to his billing as a tough guy. Most of the following is a list of some of the observations made by Mr. Holmer and the others had given to me. Was it just information or some kind of warning about the upcoming bad times? I soon found out and even added a few of my own observations to the list as well.

GABE

1. He could not complete a sentence without using profanity.
2. He never smiled. He mumbled, and seemed to always be on the verge of an explosion.
3. Gabe never spoke softly. There was no such thing as a private conversation with him. Everyone within earshot would know when he had a question or problem.
4. He never accepted responsibility for anything that happened to him, or to others when they were around him. HE was the victim and blamed others for all his problems.
5. Gabe spent a good deal of his time trying to figure out his teachers. With this information, he could then decide who is most likely to believe his excuses for not doing any homework.
6. When Gabe was served what he considered to be an unacceptable food in the cafeteria, he would get up on a table and yell his complaints so that anyone would win 100 hundred yards would know about it.
7. Gabe wore T-shirts that violated the school dress code and never seemed to understand why they were wrong.
8. Gabe finally got his driver's license. Everyone gave him plenty

of room as he entered the school parking lot. He could never understand why he couldn't park in the handicap parking spaces since he had been riding to school with a handicapped student before his license, and that was where they had ALWAYS parked.

9. He frequently asked me what would happen if he did something totally outrageous, like changing all the locks to different lockers. He wanted to know if people would be able to tell if he was high if he was wearing dark glasses.

10. Almost daily, he had some teachers, he thought should be fired. Sooner or later, his list covered almost every teacher in the school.

Gabe was not an imposing figure, at least physically. He's only about 5'7" and perhaps 130 to 140 pounds. What he lacked in size, he more than made up for in volume. When he first came to class, I asked Gabe to take a seat where I had assigned his name. Class had not been in session for five minutes and Gabe jumped into five different chairs and told me that he was not Gabe, that his name was Gabriel and that I would address him as such. I looked at Gabe for a moment, and assured him that I would grant that request. Gabe looked around the classroom, turning his head slowly from side to side, all of his "homies" is giving him the thumbs up. It was obvious he thought he got one up on me and thought I had to check my ego at his desk.

The next day Gabe evidently decided to test me a little, because he took an unassigned seat. I reminded him that, "You will sit in your assigned seat at the front of the class." His response was in his deep, resounding, baritone voice.

"I'm known for running teachers away from here, especially substitutes."

Whoa, that sounds like a threat to me. I almost laughed out loud, as I thought to myself, "I grew up in East Palo Alto, and have seen anything and everything your eyes would allow you to see, so do you think I'm going to be afraid of you?" I didn't say it, but instead decided to answer his threat with a little threat of my own. I said to him, "I've dabbled in law-enforcement and I would be making a career of it had it not been for a string of bad luck with my health." Since I wanted him to realize that education was what the class was all about, I went on to add, "If we can educate people then we won't need to arrest them because knowledge is the power to change." It must have stopped him for a moment, because he said something under his breath, then got up and sat in his assigned seat.

The following day he wanted to be called something other than Gabriel (he used his Hispanic pronunciation with emphasis on the GAH-bree-EL), but whatever the name was, I was not very successful as I tried my best to pronounce it. The whole class got a big kick out of me making a fool out of myself trying to pronounce the word. After a few tries, I finally got it together, but it seemed that Gabe had won that round again. His head was turning from side to side with the approval of all he surveyed. We seemed to manage the rest of the first week without further incident, and I was beginning to relax. That was a mistake.

At the beginning of week two I've been warned that Gabe was in a bad mood. "And you don't mess with Gabe when he's in a bad mood." He had cursed out a teacher or two. Gabe was very proud of all the negative honors that had been bestowed upon him. He had been awarded and granted the privilege of being sent to the principal office on a daily basis. That meant he would be sent to the on-campus suspension room, and when he was sent OCS he would bask in all of his splendor and all of his glory as he sat there with his arms crossed. But I had some bad news for Gabe and I decided to use the element of surprise. See, Gabe hadn't quite gotten his nerve up to curse me out yet and I wanted it to stay that way.

We avoided having a confrontation through that week, but one particular day, three weeks into the school year, I received word that this would indeed be the day. I guess you could say this would be his coming out party, and sure enough he came in upset, or at least pretending to be upset, but I wasn't buying it. I had heard him next-door giving Robert Bennin, the Special Ed math and science teacher, the blues. So I was ready, plus I was thinking I had other students I needed to concentrate on as well.

So this day Gabe came in, wanting to get the class all worked up. He asked them, "Don't you wish Mr. Riley was still here?" That was my cue. I knew it had to end there, so I asked Gabe if he would join me outside.

He seemed somewhat reluctant, and I knew he had been caught off guard. When I closed the door, I decided we would have a little man-to-man talk. I gave him first crack at me. I told him I knew he's been used to cursing out teachers and I knew that he was looking for his chance. I told him this was his chance and that it would be just between us. "You're a grown man. You'll be 20 years old soon. Go on and get it over with. I won't report you to the principal because I know this is what you want me to do. I taught in the On Campus Suspension room in Eloy for the past eight years and I refuse to send you there."

I informed him that I acted as a principal at the Eloy Junior High School for almost half the year, so I could handle whatever he wanted to dish out at me. I waited . . . and I waited. I opened the door to my classroom and I asked my aide, Carmen, if she would take over for me, since this might take a while. Then I closed the door again. Gabe seem to have lost his steam with no audience to egg him on. He had nothing to say. He was stunned by the turn of events as I robbed him of his platform. I asked if he minded if I had a few words. He muttered, "This is America, do what you want to do."

So I took my turn. I remembered something my good friend Dwayne Evans once told me, so I thought it was a perfect time to convey this message to Gabe. I told Gabe, "You can take a mule to the Kentucky Derby, but you can't make him run." I told him that at a distance, he might look like a horse, but no matter how you cut it he was still a mule! And you can't expect that mule to run with those horses. But you can expect the mule to at least trot around the track. And anything short of someone in my classroom being on a respirator, he or she was going to do some trotting. I knew that I had the chance with Gabe at that moment, because he tried his best not to laugh, and didn't succeed very well. I've always felt that if you can get a person to laugh or smile, then you always have a chance to reach them. After he stopped laughing, I asked him, "If you can't use those words in church, will you please not use them in my classroom?" He didn't answer my request, but I knew I'd given him something to think about. Guess what? Gabe never used one curse word in my class, at least not one that could be heard.

I began to look on Gabe as my diamond in the rough. Remembering my own background, I was really motivated to reach him. However, Gabe wasn't the only one. There were Francisco Lorena, John Valentine, Jed Shade, and Norman Juarez. Each and every one of these young gentlemen would stretch you to the limit. But I also realized that there are no two thumbprints exactly alike, so each had to be treated as individuals as well. I did my best to instill in them the concept that when they came into my classroom that each of them was the boss. In other words, they determined how I was going to behave. They had never been given the choice to be the boss before, but I informed them if they were seeking respect then they had to give respect in return.

I found my first high school report card and had it blown up and put on the wall. I showed them I was no different from them. It struck a chord when they pointed out to me that my report card had special education courses on it, even though my grades were A's and B's. (It's a good thing I didn't bring in an elementary school card, because there would've been nothing but D's and F's! And there was no way I wanted to motivate them to get a D).

"Hey Mr. Prince. You took special education classes," one of the students exclaimed. Bingo just what I wanted them to notice! "THAT'S MY POINT" I told them. "We can accept reasons to fail if we want to, being in special education doesn't make you dumb or stupid, we just process at a different pace."

I can never forget the many members of that first classroom class which I taught. It was just not the same as being the OCS teacher. It was lots more work, but a lot more satisfying too. There was Shari Elman, Tim Darrel, Ramsey Blount and Jessica Chavez – they made me a better teacher because they demanded the best from me. They kept me striving to make good on my promises.

Well, in spite of all the problems, which seem to come up daily, I did get through my first year at Sahuarita. My cross-country teams ran well for me, my girls' team was in the Regionals. Rene Bigness was Regional Champion, as well as All-State, and was a member of the Arizona All Star Team. In the spring, track and field rolled around, and again the girls finished second at the 3A South Regionals. Bea Alvarez was the Region 800 Champ, and Dusty Gibson was fourth in the state meet in the triple jump. The boys' team finished fourth in the region meet, with Joe Mooney and Josh Lamb going on to the state meet where they received medals. I guess you could say I had a pretty successful first year at Sahuarita, especially with athletes.

But the first year wouldn't have been the same without Gabe. It was a constant battle of push and pull to get him to grow as a student and as a person. It is strange how much he made me grow as a teacher too. On a daily basis, it was a tug of war, first one then the other of us getting the upper hand. I found that as the year progressed, I began to win more and more of the battles. I was proud of him for the progress he was making. At times, he would relapse back to the old Gabe, looking for ways to avoid hard work. Excuses were composed of whatever negative idea first came to mind, even if it made no sense at all. He once asked, "Is Mickey Mouse a cat or dog?" I had to work hard not to laugh in his in his face. He would threaten to drop out of school at least once a week because he wanted to go back to Mexico. It was rumored he wandered the streets at night in the little town of Amado, a few miles south of Sahuarita. His choice of friends was not the best. Still, progress was slow, but steady. He stopped being late for class. Jose and Jennifer got A's and so did Gabe.

I finally got him to read aloud in class, even though he first mumbled something about, "I'm not ever goin' to read this stupid book." Grudgingly he wound up participating in other things, all of which he swore never to do. He dressed up and had a senior picture taken. While he was all dressed up, he happened to go by the library, and the Librarian, Nancy Kondrat came to me with all smiles. She said she was very impressed with him. She said if I would try to get him to be in the school fashion show she was trying to have during open house for parents. I talked him into doing the fashion show, but he agreed only on the condition that I would be in it with him. He was sharp as a tack and he and I both received compliments on his being there.

Gabe had pulled the wool over most everybody's eyes for all the years he had been in school. No one thought he could read, but once I got him to open up, I couldn't seem to get him to stop. I had to actually ask him to give others a chance to read. It was really a joy to listen to his deep baritone voice because I had to admit it was pleasant to listen to him. I even told him he should be a radio announcer, because he certainly had the voice for it.

His turnaround seemed almost complete, as he was named one of the students-of-the-year by the Arizona Daily Star, the Tucson newspaper, for Sahuarita and all of Pima County. Then on the next to the last day of school, he gave me the privilege of signing his yearbook. As he sat there, he told me not to even think of trying to walk across the stage on graduation night. His comment was, "I'm not gonna walk across that stupid stage wearing some clown robe." Actually, I think he really wanted me to talk him into it, because he didn't have his usual gruff manner.

I reminded him of all we've been through together, every day a new battle, never ending. I then asked him if he wanted to hear the story about the mule again. He excused himself from the room very quickly. I ran to the door and told him if I knew he could run that fast, I would've held him back a year so he could run on my relay team.

The day of graduation, I was still not sure that Gabe would show, so I went to Mr. Holmer and told him about my fears. He laughed as he told me, "Coach, you don't need to worry because Gabe has been here since 4 o'clock pacing back and forth in front of the administration building." It seems that Gabe cared more than he had really let on to me. Graduation started at 8 PM. Gabe was dressed and ready to go by 5:30, looking nervous as a cat. As the ceremony progressed, I was impatient as I looked forward to Gabe's time to get his diploma. Finally it was time, and as his row got to their feet to do the walk-around, he and I looked at each other and gave the "thumbs up" sign. Then, when Ron Gerhart called "Gabriel W. Bustamante," there seem to be plenty of applause, although much of it may have been because of the relief of many teachers who would not have Gabe in their class ever again. As he marched off, I realized that on this 22nd day of May 1997, 30 years later, Liberation Saturday had come full circle in this man's life. It had reached another generation in the most unlikely person of Gabriel W. Bustamante.

There was a real sense of satisfaction as I reflected on the long journey from the sometimes not-so-kind streets of East Palo Alto to a little school in Sahuarita, Arizona. There was also a feeling of fulfillment too, as I realized my greatest accomplishment had come not through an Olympic medal, but through the simple act of being a teacher. For so many years, I believed God had only given me a fast pair of legs, but now I realized He had actually given me much more. He had given me a brain, and the opportunity to use it for a college education, and then in turn to pass it on to others .

That summer after Gabe graduated I really enjoyed myself, feeling very good at what had been accomplished that first year at Sahuarita. I figured from here on out things would be a piece of cake. However, it was not so. When school started again that fall, I found my great job of teaching the previous year didn't impress any of my new students. My witty sayings and interesting lessons were totally lost on the new classes. I discovered I would need to repeat that same performance again, perhaps every year for as long as I taught.

Since I had done it before, I could do it again. There were always new incidents to overcome and unwilling students with whom to work. The challenge was as great as ever.

AFTER GABE

————◆◆————

Chapter 25

The 1996–97 school year had come and gone along with the colorful Gabe and a host of others. I gained a new perspective of my role in teaching, and was looking forward to solving the many student problems that always arose.

However, life after Gabe did not get any easier. Enter Xavier "Xavi" (pronounced Ha-Vee), Mendez, Anthony "Papa" Fuentes, and oh please, let me not forget the 'very lovely' Reyna Monsivais! These students could give me a bad day without even trying. One of the problems I came across was that I always seemed to spend a lot of time with students like these. You know the old saying that the squeaky wheel is the one that gets the grease. In a way that really didn't seem fair to me, so I started making a special effort to recognize my many super young students (and athletes). I decided I would not forget to grease the un-squeaky wheel. These young men and women are just as precious and should not be overlooked.

I have to applaud the dedication of Taryn Harris, Kris Ratzlaff, Nina Zobenica, Autumn Brandt, Marcos Blanco, Josh Nelson, Tim Dagel and Jeremy Steely. These are some of my students and athletes at Sahuarita, past and present. Their dedication on and off the track was and is inspiring. In addition to their hard work in track and cross-country, they were competing to finish at the top of their classes academically. They may not have appeared to have problems, but they too needed reassurance with confidence to work at reaching their full potential. I needed them as much as they did me. Simply put, without these kids I would not have had the strength to work with those lacking in motivation. They gave and continue to give me a great sense of balance in my life.

With the passing of time comes change, and at Sahuarita there were many changes at the top. Superintendent Dr. Don Wright had passed the torch over to Assistant Superintendent, Dr. Jay, St. John. High school assistant principal Ron Gerhart had moved on, opening the door for newcomer, Steve Kellermeyer (former computer teacher, a whiz, I might add, out of Tucson's Emily Gray Junior High). Kellermeyer, who, with his boy good looks and charm came in a-blazing with his six-shooters on his hip, and a passion to keep the discipline problems in check.

Even I had begun to open up. It never seemed easy for me to make new friends, but there is something about a small school that breaks down barriers. I spent time talking more to other teachers. I now have five new friends that I can share my thoughts with from time to time. They are 9th-10th-grade counselor, Lori Jorgensen, wrestling coach Tom Dorgan, special educator Jim Phillips, and math teacher Burton Tingle. Also, conditioning and weight coach Joe Reiman is really special to me, as he has almost become my personal analyst. I told him that he should hang a shingle on his door!

I remember the lessons learned in the early days growing up in the San Francisco Bay Area from the East Palo Alto Saturday Day School, and Mrs. Wilks and the mothers for equal education in the 1960's. I continue to stay rooted in basic learning and still have a constant reminder of those Saturday lessons of one-on-one learning with Mrs. Mouton as she emphasized that Liberation Saturday never takes a day off. That meant I needed to continue my education in some way as often as possible. So recently, I decided to take a class through California State University at Hayward. The class was entitled "Motivating the unmotivated." It was just the kind of class that someone like me needs. There were certainly plenty of times that my students were definitely unmotivated. I was proud of the "A" I got, and was looking forward to using a few of the ideas in class.

Sure enough, I found a need for the class only a short time later. We were watching the movie "Twelve Angry Men" with my government development students. Parent permission slips were sent out, of course, and that meant the material might have some controversial stuff in it. The problem reared its ugly head after the two aforementioned students, Mendez and Fuentes, voiced their displeasure toward a certain member of the jury panel. Need I say the jury member was black? To say the least, things got very heated, to the point that I felt this was a personal attack on me. The particulars of the disagreement of these two stemmed from the crossing of cultural lines, resulting in a lack of respect for different points of view. I guess it is safe to say I had consciously decided to wear my feelings on my sleeve. For several days you could cut the tension in my classroom with a knife.

This stupidity on my part went on for almost two weeks. Something had to break. In my mind, this all had to do with RESPECT and PRIDE! I was thinking, "I'm the teacher and this is my classroom. I don't agree with the outburst of explicit words towards ME!" (I was thinking of myself as the juror.) To understand the students' point of view is necessary to realize that "Xavi," at six-feet-tall and a slight build of about 155 pounds, was a big man on the Sahuarita campus. He stood at or near the top of the pecking order. So for these students (especially Xavi) it was all about respect for them as well. It meant never backing down.

Fuentes stands around five-foot-five and weighs around 175-80 pounds, so he doesn't present the same as Xavi. So "Papa" was a little more on the discrete side with his demands for respect, but still was willing to stand by his good friend, Xavi. The situation had escalated to the point that I started putting extra demands on all of my students. I couldn't just ask these young men to give me more and neglect the rest of the class. I made it obvious that if you're going to pass my class you're going to have to give one hundred percent, PLUS. And then I'm still going to pour it on.

This kind of behavior could be called misplaced aggression toward the other students. I was beginning to act like one of the students, and less like a professional. I could no longer hide the anger that had festered within me.

Xavi could see that his chance of passing my class at this point was turning into "slim" or "none." So he wanted out. His first step was a trip to the 11th and 12th grade counselor Ron Boyter. Since the heat was up, he wanted out, along with Papa. Papa was holding his own, and still had a good chance of passing but he had to stand by Xavi. For both of them the only way out would be to take a correspondence course.

Xavier's next move was a visit to high school psychologist Paul Harrison. Xavi was adamant about not giving in to this teacher because he had a reputation to preserve. As far as he was concerned, there was no way he was going to apologize for his comments. He was smart enough to know something had to give, and he felt this was the only way for things to return to normal. Paul came to me and pleaded for me to come up with a solution. In some cases, when a student is in trouble, they just stop coming, so they can avoid the hassle, but that was not Xavi's way. We couldn't hide from each other because he never missed a day of school. NEVER! He was proud of his perfect attendance, and yet he was willing to give it up in order to get out of my class. It made me stop and think to myself, "I'm the educator and he's the student. On top of that, he's only 17 years old. How can I solve this and yet retain my stand on the kind of name-calling that occurred?" It had to be done in a way that retained their dignity as well. I had to also stop taking it personally, since they were just expressing an opinion.

Then I realized the answer was right in front of me. I had just completed the "Motivating the Unmotivated" class, and one of the chapters had been about role-playing. "There it is," I thought. I immediately called principal Holmer, and counselor Boyter so they would know about the plan of action that I was getting ready to take. I wanted to use the element of surprise so I decided to take a trip to Blockbuster Video, where I bought two $10 gifts certificates. Ron thought this was a great idea so we set it up that he would call both young men to his office and ask them to sit there until he got back. He then came to my room to watch my students while I went down to his office with my two $10 gift certificates. When I entered the counseling office you could tell by the looks on their faces that they did not quite know what to expect. The past two weeks had been long and tension-filled, so I wanted us all relax. The first thing I did was apologize for being three decades older and then acting as childish as I had. I got a giggle and a smile from them. Then I handed both of them the gift-wrapped certificates and told them that it wasn't much. I joked about being on a teacher's income, and they smiled. I could tell they were wondering what was coming next. When I went onto to explain that again I didn't want to tromp on their identity in order to win, they seem to finally understand.

Often times it will appear that you've lost if you only look at the present. But seeing the big picture by stepping back, it was key to the problem. It was the only way we could have a win-win. So they would get a better idea of where I was coming from, we agreed to do some role-playing. It would be for extra credit/bonus points. Papa was already doing some independent work for me anyway, so would be easy to accomplish. I decided to play the part of a disruptive student, while Papa would take the role as the teacher. Xavier would be himself, but be my partner of disruption. Papa had to agree to wear tie and be addressed as Mr. Fuentes by all the students (including me.) Further, he had to create a lesson plan for three days, even going so far as to write up a discipline notice if needed. When the three days were up, both young men would write a paper on their experiences.

Of course, I was not going to let this be a walk in the park, so the next day I was in rare form. I went to class with a bad attitude, pants sagging off my behind, shoes unlaced, hair uncombed, with a rag (my "colors") sticking out of my back pocket, and my cap cocked backwards on my head. I appeared to be a truly rebellious young man, so Mr. Holmer escorted me to class. He knocked on the door and asked Mr. Fuentes if he knew this young man. Mr. Fuentes indicated he knew me, but that he was not really happy with my truancy. Not only that, he was not pleased with me making a spectacle of myself as I entered his classroom. Needless to say, the class was in stitches with laughter. I smiled as Mr. Fuentes worked feverishly to regain control of his class. Naturally, I gravitated toward Xavier, where I sat in the seat directly in front of him. Then Xavier and I spent some time with my comments while passing candy and notes back and forth. Finally Mr. Fuentes had had enough of our disruptions so he wrote up a discipline referral.

We both wound up in Kellermeyers's office. Later I ran into Xavier at lunchtime and his comment to me was, "it was so.. perfect, so... realistic." The role-playing was so much fun and so interesting and he couldn't remember ever learning so much about a teacher in just three days. When he told me I was all right, I felt validated. You know, just another Liberation Saturday. Coming from Xavier, I realized we all had found a way to win. I put my fist in the air, and he brought his up to meet mine. We tapped our fists together, smiled and went on. By the end of the school year, Xavier and Papa were burning CDs at home for me and helping me to design greeting cards on my computer at school.

Reyna Monsivais was not to be outdone by her male counterparts. She was also at the top of the pecking order, which meant one had to walk carefully in order not to destroy her status. I realize a tough egg to crack can come in all shapes, sizes, gender and cultures. Reyna was definitely a different kind of person. She had an exotic look and rage in those deep hazel/green eyes so piercing that it could put people in their place without her having to say word. She could intimidate almost anybody with just a look. That wasn't just other students, but included teachers and administrators as well. I learned to walk gingerly around her, as we were consistently at odds on who had the role of teacher and who was the student.

I had to constantly remind her what choice of language was appropriate in the boundaries of room F231. Even after getting kicked out of my class on a bi-weekly basis she bounced back as if nothing had happened. One time she went so far as to transfer out of my English Development class. Then only a month later she wound up back in my class. She seemed to approach my personal well-being as a duty as she always made sure I was eating right. She kept me fed, but her reign of terror was always disruptive, around school and even included the bus drivers.

These pressures finally took their toll on her as she had come to a fork in the road. When she decided to transfer, I tried to convince her to stay, but no avail. In spite of our differences, one of my favorite people was moving on. By this strange twist of events I found her not really gone, just in a different place. She would still write a note and send it to me, but never allow the person bringing the note to reveal her whereabouts or what school she was attending. However, she wanted me to know that she was doing ok.

Graduation night for me is always one of life's sweetest rewards because my mind inevitably returned to those Saturday day school times, and the Liberation of going the distance. The graduation night for these three students came around. On this particular night, one of life's little surprises occurred. When Xavier received his diploma, he looked around and got my attention. Suddenly, he broke away from the line and ran over to where the teachers were sitting. He grabbed both my hands and squeezed them. Then he blurted out, "Thank you, thank you."

To which I replied, "No, thank YOU!" I wanted him to know how much he had enriched my life, but before I could say anything else, he dashed back to the line, where he was supposed to be. When the ceremonies were over, I was pleased and surprised that Xavier brought his dad and his dad's friend to meet me. His dad's message to me was, "Continue to do what you're doing. Xavier speaks highly of you and he said that your influence made the difference."

Wow! And if that weren't enough, to my surprise Reyna was waiting for me as well. She wanted me to know she had gotten her diploma. Now sitting in my room is a 5x7 photo of Reyna, clad and cap and gown as she is shaking hands and receiving her diploma. She sent the photo special delivery with a note: "To my favorite teacher, WE MADE IT!"

Recently, we had a coaches' get together, and I visited with one of my assistant coaches, "Tavo" Blanco. Yes, he is the same Tavo, who played a role in my going to Sahuarita. We had a good laugh over his always asking me if I was going to come and be his coach, even though he knew he was graduating. It was almost as if he knew beforehand I would someday hire him as my assistant. He asked me how the book was coming, and I told him we were just cleaning up the last chapter or so. He then asked me, "Coach, the book isn't really about you being a fast runner, is it?" And, of course, he's right; it isn't. It is a continuing story of one life touching another, which then goes on to touch another. Tavo demonstrated as much this past spring, as he coached our senior class salutatorian to a second place in the state meet in the discus event. Brian Zukowski was only so-so in the discus just the year before, but Tavo spent hours and hours working to get the best from him. It may seem like a long way from East Palo Alto, but I can see in Brian the hard work and dedication of those Liberation Saturday teachers from many years ago.

I reflect on a simple movie of Twelve Angry Men, which turned into a saga of Fifteen Angry Men. I began to realize that negative baggage is not limited to this particular campus as it hangs out at every school campus Anywhere, USA. It's like a revolving door, repeating itself over and over. It comes disguised always looking for an opening through the baggage of self-doubt, deep-rooted, anger, depression, disruptive and abusive home life, no home life, peer pressures. This revolving door certainly has no particular age limit, and does not discriminate against gender, culture, or economic backgrounds. Many times it is a person just searching to belong, having been misplaced academically, misrepresented as to abilities, or just plain misdiagnosed or even a symptom of a confused state of loneliness. Sadly, many of them never find their Liberation Saturday.

But hanging out on the other end of the campus are the true unsung heroes that deliver every day, every week, every school year. Call them the Deliverance Center Group, The Liberators, whatever. I've had the blessings of headlines and glory so I can accept the relative anonymity of teaching. Most educators pass through their careers without their fifteen minutes of fame. It is exciting to realize one person has the power to change a life, and sometimes is blessed enough to touch more than one. I have the utmost admiration for the Heroes Without Headlines that provide the backbone of American Education. The power of liberation starts with One Seed Planted. Liberation should not be limited to those Saturday Day Schools. Liberation is a twenty-four hour/seven-day process, a lifelong commitment!

We are all educators. The power is within us all!

FAVORITE MEMORIES

Chapter 26

At the indoor Long Beach Muhammad Ali Invitationals meet, Maxi Parks and I went to Queen Mary and met Olympic Gold Medal winners Wilma Rudolph and Muhammad Ali. Ali shook my hand and told me, "You're ugly. You ain't as pretty as me. You ain't as pretty as me." He got no argument from me. Maxi busted out laughing.

When I was about 12 years old, I was shopping in downtown Palo Alto when Shirley Temple Black stepped out of her husband's office to the street right in front of me. She started talking to me and I recognized her from TV. She asked me what grade I was in and told me, "Education is so important! Make sure you learn something every day in school." She made me feel like she had known me my whole life.

I was so proud the day my daughter Diamond graduated from high school. She was awarded a certificate for Perfect Attendance from Pre-School all the way through High School.

When I was 13 years old, a friend and I were trying to learn how to do the new "Fosbury Flop". We were practicing by jumping over the neighbor's hedges. We had an audience because folks were outside doing summer activities. A golden haired lady came out of the house where she was visiting her aunt. She told us to stop jumping over the hedges. We didn't stop. So she came outside and swatted us on the bottom, playfully, but it had some sting on it. Then she told us, "Now go tell Mama that!" Everyone started laughing but we didn't know why. Someone told us that the golden haired lady had just had a new hit record out called "Tell Mama". Her name was Etta James!

I filled in for Herman Frazier at a speaking engagement in Tempe, Arizona at the Kiwanis Park. Also on the agenda was then Congressman John McCain. The Congressman was so impressed with my story in the East Valley Magazine that he told me he was going to give his copy of the magazine to Governor Bruce Babbit. I never thought twice about it. A few weeks later, I received a shock in the mail. Governor Babbit sent me a personally signed letter thanking me for telling my story and recognizing all my hard work.

I was at a speaking engagement at a church in Casa Grande, Arizona with heavyweight boxer, Earnie Shavers. Afterward, the congregation took us out to the Golden Corral on Florence Ave. Between me and Earnie, we almost ate them out of food!

I was 19 years old and still didn't know how to drive. I went on a trip with my Cal Poly roommate/teammate Stephen Oren Converse from Reseda, CA, to the Hearst Castle which was about an hour away. He asked me if I still didn't know how to drive and I told that Mr. Beck in East Palo Alto said I was hopeless and he was pulling his hair out at the end.

So Stephen pulled over and told me, "You're driving the rest of the way." What a wild wild ride that was!

I had traveled with my Fresno Pacific team to the Westmont College meet even though I was too sick to compete. The Cal Lutheran sprinter, LaVannes Rose, approached me and said, "I heard what you're going through and I don't know what to say to you, except, "Just Hang, man." He said it with such sincerity for someone so young and especially from someone I didn't know. Those words echoed in my mind during the darkest times of my fight. When I was so low, I would hear him saying, "Just hang, man."

Due to a miscommunication between me and AIA Head Coach Lloyd Jackson, I was unable to join the team when they left for Europe. But fate stepped in and Wheaton College coach, Don Church, who was heading up the USA Team going to Europe reached out to me and invited me to join his team. You should have seen the look on Coach Jackson's face when we ran into each other at the hotel in Belgrade. But I did thank him for helping me get my passport. We both had a good laugh at that.

The first time I saw my Ravenswood high school classmate, Mike McCurry, standing and delivering a speech on the steps of the White House serving as President Clinton's White House Press Secretary.

My best high school friend Roy Lee Williams' son, "Little Roy", played safety for the University of Oklahoma, and went on to play for the Dallas Cowboys. Roy Lee helped me make a dream come true for one of my students we affectionately called "Cholo". His dream was to one day meet his favorite NFL player Emmitt Smith. He was hanging out with some kids that concerned me and I wanted to keep him motivated to stay in school.

So I told him that I could get him to Emmitt Smith but that he had to keep his grade up in my class. He looked at me like I had a third eyeball. I ended up taking him to the Arizona Cardinals vs the Dallas Cowboys game in Glendale, AZ. Little did Cholo know that I had pre-arranged with Roy Lee to be seated in the area where the players families' gather after the game. Well, let me tell you, when Little Roy brought Emmitt Smith right over to Cholo, I think Cholo stopped breathing. He got a photo with Emmitt Smith and Little Roy and got autographs! He wasn't just walking on cloud nine – he floating above it. Years later, while eating ice cream with friends at the local Dairy Queen, Cholo walked over to our table and introduced his mother, his wife, and his baby daughter. He wanted to tell me that if it hadn't been for me, he would either be in jail or dead. I felt like I got the air knocked out of me – I was stunned. His mother was crying and just kept repeating, "Thank you, thank you, thank you."

My team was getting ready to compete at the Arizona State Track and Field meet when I had heard from my legendary friend, Herman "BB" Andrews, National Hall of Fame inductee for being one of the winningest high school track and field coaches in America, and his son, Herman Jr. They said they will have a big surprise waiting for me at the meet. And they were right. Much to my astonishment, they had brought with them the great Jessie Owen's 1936 Gold Medals with them. I was privileged to be able to hold all four of them in the palms of hands. I'm still smiling!

I was still trying to master computer skills as a teacher at Sahuarita High School. My principal at the time was Dave Holmer. He spent countless hours teaching me the difference between SAVE and SAVE AS on the computer. That poor man's hair probably fell out, but I finally got it. Thank you for saving me hours of retyping reports!

My 2 Dr. V's:

1) For 23 years I have been having breakfast with Olympic coach, Dr. Joe I. Vigil every Tuesday. He has been treating me to hash-browns and iced coffee latte the whole time. Oh the stories we share!

2) I clearly remember the day in that my Superintendent, Dr. Manny O. Valenzuela, came to me very excited about some important news to tell me. He informed me that I was being honored by Brooks Athletic as one of the Top 25 Most Inspirational Coaches in America. I was so overwhelmed because I knew that I had been chosen from over 8,000 nominations.

My dear friend and fellow track coach, Ricardo "Rick" Robles, reminisce about our dining adventure's at Mel's Hamburgers in San Manuel, Arizona after track meets anytime we talk to each other.

At a school presentation, the Sahuarita High School Athletic Director, Chris Fanning, was the one that presented me with the Bronze Shoe from Brooks Athletic and the check for $6000 worth of equipment. I was honored to have the short documentary of my life that was filmed by Dave Verwys and Richard Knapp shown at the San Diego Black Film Festival in 2008.

In 2015 and 2016 I had the honor of coaching back-to-back Arizona high school State Runners-Up girls and boys track and field teams. This included the amazing 4x400 meter relay team of Emily Blevin, Yasheika Beckaroo, Melissa Williams, and Tyler McClelland. Their time was 3:53.67 which was one of the top 50 times in the nation at the time for schools that medaled. They all broke their school records in that race. This also included Tanner Dougle Division 3 Runner of the Year, and Allyn Williams, Division 3 Athlete of the Year. I had purchased Allyn a pair of orange track shoes on sale for $.39 at Ross in the bargain bin. He jumped 23'3½". That is the same year I was awarded Coach of the Year by the Arizona Daily Star newspaper. We achieved our trifecta!

In 1984 in my final race, I won the Arizona TAC Open 100 meter. Not the Olympics but I go out a winner!

When I was in high school, I defended a young man from a beating. I didn't know him well, I just knew it wasn't fair and I understood what it was like to be treated unfairly. I called him Danny Partridge because that's who he reminded me of. 35-years later, my old high school coach, Tommie Smith, was coming to Tucson for a "Sports Extravaganza" that Olympic hurdler, LaTanya Sheffield, was hosting. He called the Arizona Daily Star newspaper and told them that they should put me on the front page because he had just finished reading my book. So the editor put a story together that explained how Tommie Smith and I knew each other. Also in attendance at the Extravaganza was the James Beard's award-winning chef Janas Wilder. Turns out, Janas lived in Tucson and read the newspaper. A reporter at the event, Jesse Vanderson, asked me how I knew Janas. I said, "The only Janas I know is the restaurant I can't afford to eat at." Well Janas came straight over to me and said, "You might not remember me . . ." but he couldn't finish the sentence because he got choked up. I realized that I did know him and I told him, "You're Danny Partridge." His reaction was so genuine because he knew that I was the only who called him that. His eyes welled up and as he hugged me. His wife told me that he had practically levitated off the bed when he saw my picture on the front page. He turned to the crowd and told them that I was his protector in high school.

At that same event, John Carlos, the Olympian that stood on the platform with Tommie Smith, and I gave a clinic on how to come out of the starting blocks. Carlos was walking around with my book in his pocket. What a day that was for me!

After the Extravaganza, I was so honored that Latonya asked me to write a letter to nominate her daughter, Jade, for the Arizona Gatorade, track and field athlete of the year. I am so happy to report: Jade won!

There was a program through Ohio State University where they recognized outstanding teachers from around the nation. My principal at the time, Mark Neish, nominated me for that award. He said my teaching method was out-of-the-box which is exactly what my students needed.

I was so proud when 200-meter Bronze medalist Dwayne Evans and his wife Lori, asked me to stand with them with their baby daughter Turquoise at her christening. I was never so humbled!

Gary Curtis Davis, a future Miami Dolphin, and I were watching my cousin, Wayne Moore, during the 1972 Super Bowl with the Miami Dolphins. My cousin started at left tackle as number 79 and that team is the only team in NFL history to go undefeated the whole season, 17-0.

After my appearance on the 700 Club, Pastor R. Snell and Minister Wiley asked me to give my first ever speaking engagement at the Miracle Temple Church on Monticello Ave. in Jersey City, NJ. I told them that I wasn't a speaker but that I'd do my best. I was so scared I almost passed out.

Fresno Pacific/Athletes in Action pole vaulter, Steve Hardison, convinced Athletes in Action Head Coach, Lloyd Jackson, to recruit me as a member of Athletes in Action. I received a letter inviting me to join the team in Santa Ana. I drove as fast as I could before he changed his mind.

There was a radio program on KDIA out of San Francisco that reached East Palo Alto that I listened to every Sunday night. The program was Preacher King Louis H. Narcisse. I loved hearing him say, "It's nice to be nice and it's nice to let the people know that you're nice!" This was my favorite thought!

Every time I smell Tabu perfume, I'm brought back to the California Track and Field State Meet at UCLA when my Big Mama Lois brought my mother Mildred to meet me for the first time since I was toddler. It is a warm and happy feeling that always catches me by surprise.

GOING THE DISTANCE

Chapter 27

As a member of AIA, I participated in Invitational meets, shared our stories with people and gave track clinics at the junior high, high school and junior college Level. The following year I found myself on a six week tour in Eastern Europe competing at Stadion Evzena Rosickeho, Prague in Czechoslovakia and surprisingly being front page news in Belgrade, Yugoslavia. How did I get here? Sharing the nerves and emotions with my teammates on foreign soil took me to a place I still can't describe, but I will hold dear forever. I had finally come of age where I was starting to share my feelings with other people. I can still hear my friends, Fran and Dorothy, who I've known since kindergarten, saying, "Trust the journey."

Twelve years would go by as I pursued teaching certificates in Special Education and Elementary Education. After countless interviews I was finally offered a teaching position as On Campus Suspension Teacher. My professional career had begun!

Fast forward to Spring of my eighth year of teaching: it was the last five weeks of the school year, five weeks that would shape the rest of my professional career. I was asked if I would take over as Acting Principal. Life appears to have come full circle from my first day of kindergarten and the tinker toy closet. I would go on to teach and coach for another 25 years.

I now realize that nothing happens before its time. I really had to learn how to wait and be patient on things. What matters more than anything is not how smart you are or what your aspirations are, it's how strong your desire is to be at your best. All things happen in their own time, but this still doesn't give the license to procrastinate. Life is just like the descriptions in the chapters in this book. Fight to be better than what people expect you to be. Regardless of how we carry out our travels, passing through triumphs, illness, developmental differences, despair or merely being misunderstood, we all deserve a sense of belonging, a reason to strive for purpose and success. As paraphrased from the documentary The Boy Whose Skin Fell Off, which touched me deeply, "I believe that we all are placed on this earth to learn lessons. Earth is the classroom; it teaches us to learn to deal with frustration as well as to overcome disappointment." Despite life's difficulties we can learn the value of "going the distance." That's the thing that separates us from being just your average Joe.

Joseph E. Prince

Thank you for reading...

NOT YOUR AVERAGE

151

Cover Design

by

Alya Hurych

In the back of the bus is Joe's Uncle Chester, who has been on this life journey with Joe from the start. Through triumph and tragedy, he's never been too far away and has stayed on the bus to support Joe on his incredible journey of going the distance.

Got an idea for a book? Contact Curry Brothers Publishing, LLC. We are not satisfied until your publishing dreams come true. We specialize in all genres of books, especially religion, leadership, family history, poetry, and children's literature. There is an African Proverb that confirms, "When an elder dies, a library closes." Be careful who tells your family history. Ensure their values are your family's values? Our staff will navigate you through the entire publishing process and we take pride in going the extra mile in meeting your publishing goals.

Improving the world one book at a time!

CURRY BROS.
MARKETING + PUBLISHING GROUP

Curry Brothers Publishing, LLC, PO Box 247 Haymarket, VA 20168
Office: (888) 726-1828
Visit us at www.currybrotherspulishing.com